CRITICAL LESSONS
In SLAVERY
And The SLAVETRADE

DTR 360 Books

www.DTR360Books.com
IG: @DTR360Books_

CRITICAL LESSONS
In SLAVERY
And The SLAVETRADE

Essential Studies and Commentaries On Slavery, In General, and the African Slavetrade, In Particular

Co-authored and Edited by

John Henrik Clarke

Professor Emeritus, African and Puerto Rican Studies, Hunter College

ILLUSTRATED

Truth & Sanity Reprint Series Is An Imprint of

Native Sun Publishers
Richmond
1996

All **Native Sun Publishers** books, including this one, are printed (and/or re-printed) on acid-free paper to ensure the survivability of our Works.

The publisher and special adjunct editor would like to thank Prof. Clarke's assistant, Sister Ann, for her cooperation in getting this work completed; and, in a similar vein, we would like to thank our satellite office in D.C. and its head, the Nightrider, for its/her work as well.

International Standard Book Numbers
1-879289-06-7 (C)   1-879289-07-5 (P)
Library of Congress Catalogue Card Number: 96-68505

Newly Expanded and Revised Second Edition

Second Printing

Manufactured in the United States of America

Native Sun   **Publishers**

P.O. Box 13394, Richmond, VA 23225

DEDICATED

to

Anna Swanston, Secretary, friend and colleague
for service over and beyond the call of duty,

and

her family — Stephenie, Brandt and Ndeye.

CONTENTS

ACKNOWLEDGEMENT

The basic contents of this book were prepared as lectures in the CBS/TV educational series, *African Heritage: The Story of Black America*. Most of the topics for discussion and activities which appear at the end of each lecture were developed by Dr. Carolyn Fowler, formerly of Clark Atlanta University. The community representatives and consultants for the TV series were professors Vincent Harding, William Strickland and John Henrik Clarke. The publication of these lectures was originally projected as a ten volume set and unfortunately like most ambitious schemes, this one never materialized. The first volume was prepared but never published; however, the second volume was prepared and published. In republishing this the second volume at this time, I have taken into consideration the fact that a wealth of new and exciting material on the slave trade has been published in the more than two decades since it first appeared. In the Foreword and the Commentary I have reviewed some of the best of this new material in order to call attention to its significance and to bring the book more up-to-date. I have not altered any material in the original volume. I have, nonetheless, compiled a new and more relevant bibliography.

FOREWORD

In 1992, with the 500 year celebration of
Christopher Columbus' voyages to what is referred to
as the New World, there was a renewed interest in
the expansion of Europe, outside of Europe, that had
begun in the fifteenth and sixteenth centuries and a
revaluation of what that expansion set in motion for
the world's nations, history, and peoples. Most of
the people on earth would be influenced by this
expansion, both for the good and for the bad. The
influence on African people was the most negative
and the most tragic because the Africans were the
least prepared for the disruption it caused.

Had the European interest and entry into Africa
been delayed for fifty or one hundred years, there
might not have been any slavery at all. There had
been difficulties developing between African states
in coastal West Africa and the African states in
coastal East Africa at the time. European presence
in West Africa and the Arab presence in East Africa
accentuated the differences between these African
states. Both the Europeans and the Arabs played
the same cruel game against the Africans. Using

different methods and different circumstances, they put one African group against another and eventually ended up by conquering both groups.

The Arabs had built a number of large settlements along the coast of East Africa with the cooperation of the Africans. By the fifteenth century the Arabs were turning on their former African friends and enslaving them. Later the Portuguese moving up the coast of East Africa from the south met the Arabs moving down the coast from the north and they combined their respective slave trades. Large numbers of these slaves were shipped to Brazil, other parts of South America and the Caribbean Islands.

In West Africa, the Portuguese and the Spaniards dominated the early slave trade. The Danish and the Swedish came late into the trade and remained mostly middle-men. Because of some difference of opinion with the Catholic Church, England was also late in entering the slave trade. However, when England entered, late and furious, the sloppy business of slavery became a business in every sense of the word. It now had procedures, territorial assignments (for slave-catching), and a code of conduct (between slave-catchers and sellers) that was expected to be adhered to.

In East Africa, the last of the great trading states were in some kind of disarray. These states were used as trading posts by the Africans and the Arabs at a time when a more friendly relationship existed between the two.

In inner West Africa, sometimes referred to as the Western Sudan, a number of great sovereign states had flourished. The last of these states was Songhay. This state was invaded by a combination of European, Arab and African troops in 1591. The wreck and ruin wrought by this invasion facilitated the spread of the slave trade inland. This period was also a turning point in the history of the world. Europe was emerging from the lethargy of the Middle Ages. It was regaining its confidence, manifesting a new form of nationalism and extending that nationalism into racism. The Africans had goods and services that the European

iv

needed, and the European had the basic technology that the African needed. Had the African needs and the European needs been considered on an equal basis there could have been an honest exchange between African and European and the African could have gained the technology needed and the European could still have had labor in large numbers without the slave trade and the massive destruction of humanity that went into the slave trade. This idea, only a dream in the minds of a few men, could have changed the world for the better had it been seriously considered.

The concept of slavery was not new to Africa. Various African nations and societies had known a form of slavery by this time. This slavery consisted mainly of indentured servitude, the use of prisoners-of-war as slave labor and some small tribal African nations coming under the protection of larger more powerful African nations. These indentured slaves engaged in farming, cattle-raising and sometimes served as shock troops in the armies of the dominant nations. Their families were not broken-up and a large number of them were permitted to have their own farms and own cattle. This system of slavery in no way resembled the system of chattel slavery developed by the European in Africa.

The concept of slavery was not new to Europe either. Europeans had experienced a thousand years of internal slavery before the start of the Atlantic slave trade. The internal slavery in Europe was called Feudalism, and this was slavery in its truest sense because most of the population did not have the right to determine their own destiny. The people were controlled and manipulated by the sloppy politics of Europe and the Catholic Church. During this period there had been an internal struggle between European nations. Europe had drained its treasuries and taxed its human resources in a romanticized charade called the Crusades. After the Crusades, Europe experienced famine and a drain on its human resources caused by diseases they had never previously known, and which were now out of control. When Europeans awakened to the nightmare of their existence they began to search for land,

food, new energy and new resources beyond their
shores. Their knowledge of Asia and Africa was
limited to legend and tall tales, but they suspected
that there was a source of food and other resources
beyond their shores. With an improvement in their
maritime skills, they set out to find this new food
supply and whatever resources they could find. In
their search for Asia and the treasures they
believed existed there, they found Africa.

When the Europeans discovered the African
presence in the world for the second time, the
first time being during the Greco-Roman period,
their attitude toward African people had changed.
To understand this change we must deal with the
reshaping of the European mind in the years between
1400 and 1600. In their religious and political
wars many Europeans had lost all sentimental
attachment to themselves. They had emerged from the
Middle Ages people poor, land poor, and resource
poor. A large number of their population had been
lost in plagues and famines, and the Crusades had
awakened Europe to the world beyond its shores and
the many creature comforts that had not at that
time reached Europe. They were beginning to regain
the lost concept of longitude and latitude and
re-discovering maritime skill mainly from information preserved by Africans and Arabs at the
University of Salamanca in Spain. The best of this
information had come to them from China, the
leading maritime nation of that day. Europeans,
were also, at that time, searching for a route to
mainland Asia in order to obtain the sweets, and
spices, some legendary some real, that they needed
for the European food of that day, which was often
unpalatable.

Once they regained the knowledge essential for
maritime survival, they began to build the ships
that could endure long voyages. Skills in shipbuilding continued to develop until shipbuilding
became a new and major industry in Europe. A large
number of these ships were employed in the slave
trade, and the slave trade across the Atlantic
became an industry in itself. This industry in turn
spurred other industries and subsequently changed

the economic picture of the whole world. It is not an exaggeration to say that the European slave trade to Africa rescued Europe and its economy from the ravages of the Middle Ages.

Early in the history of man there was no name for the human condition we refer to as slavery because no one had ever been relegated to that condition. The circumstances that would create the condition did not exist and the idea had never influenced a single mind. The enslavement of one people by another, in my opinion, grew out of fear, need and greed. In order to appease the conscience of the enslaver, a rationale had to be created — the enslaver had to convince himself and his victim that this new condition placed the victim and his family outside of the realm of humanity. The Moslems and the European Christians of the fifteenth and sixteenth centuries found no difficulty in finding a rationale for their involvement in the slave trade. As early as the seventh century the Arabs had invaded Africa with a vengeance. This invasion was part religious and part a raiding expedition. Roman domination in North Africa and Roman taxation and mismanagement of the early Christian Church, before and after the Conference at Nicea, made the Africans become disenchanted with the Roman presence in their country. The Africans had assumed that by welcoming the Arabs and accepting Islam they would relieve themselves of the yoke of Roman domination. In their political naivete they did not understand that the Arabs were replacing Roman domination in the name of Islam and that their rule over them would differ from the Romans only in methodology.

The slave trade in East Africa gave the Arabs a place in the new economic sun until they were challenged by the Europeans. The Arab slave trade in East Africa had started over one thousand years before the European slave trade. The Arab slave trade and the Arabs themselves have rarely, if ever, been examined with any degree of thoroughness, nor have the Arab concept of Islam and the European concept of Christianity been seen as the religions of conquerors. The religion of the conqueror is nearly always used as the handmaiden

vii

and rationale for his conquest, and no conqueror has ever come to Africa to do African people any good. To understand this you have to remove certain standard misconceptions from your mind, permanently.

In less than a generation after the Arabs entered Africa, a treaty had been imposed on the people of the Sudan called the Bagt Treaty in which the people of the Sudan were to deliver three hundred and sixty slaves to the Arabs in the north annually. In his book, *Nubia, Corridor to Africa,* William Y. Adams refers to the Bagt Treaty in this manner:

Covenant from the Amir Abd Allah ibn Sa'd ibn Abi Sarh to the king of the Nubians and to all the people of his kingdom; a covenant binding upon great and small among the Nubians from the frontier of the land of Aswan to the border of the land of Alwa. Abd Allah ibn Sa'd ibn Abi Sarh has established it for them as a guarantee and a truce to be effective among them and the Moslems of Upper Egypt who live adjacent to them, as well as other Moslems and client peoples (dhimmis; i.e. Christians and Jews). Verily, you are communities of Nubia enjoying the guarantee of Allah and that of His Messenger Mohammed, the Prophet; with the condition that we shall not wage war against you, nor declare war against you, nor raid you, as long as you abide by the stipulations which are in effect between us and you. (Namely) that you may enter our territories, passing through but not taking up residence in them, and we may enter yours through but not taking up residence in them. You are to look after the safety of any Moslem or ally (of the Moslems) who lodges in your territories or travels in them, until he departs from you.

You are to return every slave of the Moslems who runs off to you, sending him back to the land of Islam. You are to return any Moslem engaged in hostilities against the other Moslems, who seeks refuge with you. You are to send him forth from your territories to the land of Islam, neither inclining to (help) him nor preventing him from (returning).

You are to look after the mosque which the Moslems have built in the courtyard of your capital, and you are not to prevent anyone from worshipping in it, or interfere with any Moslem who goes to it and remains in its sanctuary until he departs from it. And you are to sweep it, keep it lighted, and honor it.

Each year you are to deliver 360 slaves which you will pay to the Imam of the Moslems from the finest slaves of your country, in whom there is no defect. (They are to be) both male and female. Among them (is to be) no decrepit old man or woman or any child who has not reached puberty. You are to deliver them to the Wali of Aswan.

It shall not be incumbent upon any Moslem to defend (you) against any enemy who attacks you or to prevent him on your behalf from doing so, from the frontier of the land of Alwa to the land of Aswan.

If you do harbour a slave belonging to a Moslem, or kill a Moslem or ally, or if you expose to destruction the mosque which the Moslems have built in the courtyard of your capital, or you withhold any of the 360 slaves, this truce and guarantee which we and you have equally set down will be void, 'so that God will judge between us' — 'and He is the Best of Judges.'

Incumbent upon us hereby is observance of the pact of God and His agreement and His good faith, and the good faith of His Messenger Mohammed. And incumbent upon you toward us is the utmost observance of the good faith of the Messiah and that of the Disciples and of any of the people of your religion and community whom you reverence. God be the witness of that between us.

In spite of the pious tone of this quote from the Treaty, it is clear neither Arabs, nor any other invader, came to Africa to do Africa any good. A brief look at how and why the Arabs invaded Africa is in order at this point. The following explanation is taken from J.C. deGraft Johnson's book, *African Glory*. He says:

The Arab conquest of North Africa was no walkover, except perhaps in Egypt, where the Arabs were received as deliverers from the cruel rule of Byzantium.

The resistance put up by Kuseila of Mauritania

and by his relative Kahina reflected the African mood of the period. In fact, so fierce and determined were the African counter-attacks that an Arab governor once remarked that the conquest of Africa was impossible; and that scarcely had a Berber tribe been exterminated when another came to take its place. However, after Kahina's defeat and death in 705 African resistance eventually weakened.

Hassan bin Numan, now Arab governor of Egypt, was able to rebuild the third holy city of the Moslems, which had been destroyed a few years earlier by Kuseila, but it was Musa ibn Nusair, the successor of Hassan bin Numan in 708, who carried out the final conquest of North Africa. He conquered the whole of Morocco, except Ceuta (Count Julian, governor of Ceuta, was able to repel the Arab forces and keep his territory independent of Arab rule, as will be seen), and this gave him command of the western route to the Sudan.

From the above it is clear that the Arabs entered Africa as conquerors and not as liberators. Many deceived Africans converted to Islam and joined the Arabs in their military aspirations in Spain and in the Mediterranean. This is still a little-known aspect of African-Arab relationships; and the partial cooperation and collaboration between the Africans and the Arabs would last nearly eight hundred years, ending on the eve of 1492. This period is graphically described in John G. Jackson's book, *Introduction to African Civilizations*, in the chapter, "Africa and the Civilizing of Europe". Also see a book by Bernard Lewis, *The Arabs and The Discovery of Europe* and a book published by The Arab Information Center called, *The Arab Inheritance of Western Civilization*. This period was the preface to the Atlantic slave trade.

A human trait in the African culture would now work to their disfavor. Throughout most of their history, Africans have been hospitable to strangers. Their first contact with the European in coastal West Africa was friendly. They did not know the European intention at that time. Slavery was already an old institution before the European came to Africa. A system of servitude had been a part of the life of some West African nations.

x

However, the system of chattel slavery and forced migration introduced by the Europeans was alien to the African way of life and became the best known and best recorded slave period in the history of the world. It also became, in my opinion, the most tragic period and a turning point in the history of the world. The neglected tragedy of this system is that it did not have to occur at all. Had the European entered into a genuine partnership with the African, instead of reducing them to slavery, there would have been more goods and services to be had, both for the Europeans and the Africans, through contract labor.

Let us examine briefly the myth of an invading people spreading civilization to another people. People never spread civilization to other people; they spread their way of life at the expense of the other people's culture. Both the Europeans and the Arabs and the other invaders of Africa declared war on every form of African culture and spiritual way of life. Many conquerors remained in Africa for hundreds of years without learning one word of an African language or showing any respect for an African traditional way of life. In this respect the Arabs and Islam are as guilty as the Europeans and their Christianity. For further insight on this subject I suggest that you read, *The Colonization of Africa by Alien Races*, by Sir Harry Johnston, and *East Africa and Its Invaders*, by Reginald Copeland. Near the end of the nineteenth century the Caribbean scholar, Edward W. Blyden, wrote a book on this subject that still has some value for us today. The book is entitled, *Christianity, Islam and the Negro Race*.

In spite of the many points of view on this tragic story, there are still some missing dimensions. The argument over statistics will go on indefinitely because the numbers are far more extensive than what most people are willing to believe. The Nigerian writer, Joseph E. Inikore, in his book, *Forced Migration*, had made a reassessment of the statistics on slavery in the United States. Sterling Stuckey, in his book, *Slave Culture*, called our attention to the impact slavery had on the transplanted culture of Africans under pressure and in transition. Professor Stuckey maintains that African culture survived in spite of the protracted assault on it in the Americas and on the Caribbean Islands. This is the theme put forth by Melville Herskovitz in his book, *The Myth of the Negro Past*. The senior writer on this subject, in the years after 1915 and the founder of the Association For the Study of African American Life and History, is Carter G. Woodson. His major works on the subject are, *African Background Outlined*, and *The Education of the Negro Prior to 1861*. Both were republished recently and are again available in the bookstores. These two books need to be read again because, unfortunately, African people in the United States still have some misconceptions about their education and education in general. They are under the assumption that they were brought to the United States, or to the so-called New World, to be elevated and educated, when in fact their sole purpose for being brought here was to become a part of a massive labor force. Professor Inikore reexamines the situation in the following manner. In *Forced Migration*, he starts the story at its very beginning; he says:

The export slave trade from Africa began early in the Christian era with exports to the Muslim world through the Sahara, the Red Sea and the Indian Ocean. By the ninth century A.D., the annual volume of exports to the Muslim world had become quite significant, and continued so up to the nineteenth century. For the period up to the fifteenth century the Muslim territories around the Mediterranean and beyond were the main slave importing regions of the world, fed by supplies both from Europe and from sub-Saharan Africa. In the fifteenth and sixteenth centuries Western European countries led by Portugal and Spain embarked upon voyages of exploration which gave rise to the establishment of European colonies in parts of the Atlantic territories and Indian Ocean islands. The great need for labour to exploit the resources of these colonies added a new sector to the export slave trade from Africa — the trans-Atlantic slave trade. The new branch quickly came to supersede the older one in annual export volume. For over four centuries both sectors of the trade went on simultaneously, removing millions of persons — men, women and children — from sub-Saharan Africa.

In the creation and the search for a rationale for their slave trade, Europeans had to literally mortgage their announced spirituality in order to place the African outside of the realm of humanity and the grace of God. When they converted the African to their concept of Christianity most of them could not accept an African Christian as their equal.

Slavery had now become a three continent industry that would change the economic and commercial picture of the world. The tremendous drain on the time, energy and the human resources of Europe found remedy in the Atlantic slave trade and the expansion of Europe into what was referred to as the New World. The building of massive slave forts and castles along the west coast of Africa made slavery a vital part of the new western economic system. No matter what the African did or did not do in the slave trade, this unfortunate business succeeded because of the European's new understanding of maritime skills, the development of gun technology and a class of slave traders who had no human feeling toward other people. The involvement of the African in this trade was effective; however, the African did not have the ships nor the connections that would have given them control over the massive industry that the slave trade became.

The life aboard the slave ships was high and tragic drama. Although most of the crew of these ships were the scum of European society, some could only tolerate one voyage; others later left the trade in order to save their sanity. The captured Africans were in continuous rebellion — both the captives and the crew were in danger throughout these voyages. Life aboard these ships was pure hell, for both.

The arrival of the Africans in what is referred to as the New World would change the whole world. The establishment of the plantation system in the

New World was the establishment of a way of life for the European that had not previously existed. The Africans' encounter with the Indigenous Natives, mistakenly referred to as "Indians," was another high drama in their forced migration.

The African slave trade is understated and often missing from the pages of world history; however, the history of the world will be out of kilter until the African slave trade is seen and understood, in all of its dimensions and reverberations, both past and present.

John Henrik Clarke
June, 1996

INTRODUCTION

In this, the second book in the Black Heritage Series, the participating writers have reopened and reexamined a much written about subject that is still misunderstood by most people. The basis of this misunderstanding is in the fact that most students of this subject look upon the African slave trade as though it were the only system of slavery known to man. Slavery is an old institution and there are no people who have not at some time in history been a victim of it.

The African slave trade can best be understood if we at least take a brief look at the historical roots of slavery as a world institution.

Slavery in ancient society was appreciably different from the type of slavery that was introduced into Africa by the Europeans in the fifteenth and sixteenth centuries. In most ancient societies the slave was held in servitude for a limited time, for specific reasons, and, in most cases, the slaves were captured in local wars. Skin color was not a factor as to whether a person did or did not become a slave and, in most cases, the slave had some rights that the master had to respect. In ancient Egypt, Kush, Greece, and early Rome there were clearly defined codes of conduct governing the relationship between the slaves and their masters. Some of the earliest of these codes are recorded in the laws of Moses.

In the book, *The History of Slavery and the Slave Trade*, by W.O. Blake, published in 1858, the following information relating to early slavery is revealed:

> The Mosaic institutions were rather predicated upon the previous existence of slavery in the surrounding nations, than designed to establish it for the first time; and the provisions of the Jewish law upon this subject, effected changes and modifications which must have improved the condition of slaves among that particular people. There were various modes by which the Hebrews might be reduced to servitude. A poor man might sell himself; a father might sell his children; debtors might be delivered as slaves to their creditors; thieves who were unable to make restitution for the property stolen were sold for the benefit of the sufferers. Prisoners of war were subjected to servitude; and if a Hebrew captive was redeemed by another Hebrew from a Gentile, he might be sold to another Israelite. At the return of the year of jubilee all Jewish captives were set free. However, by some writers it is stated that this did not apply to foreign slaves held in bondage; as, over those the master had entire control.
>
> The law of Moses provides that "if a man smite his servant or his maid with a rod, and he die under his hand he shall be surely punished." This restriction is said, by some, to have applied only to Hebrew slaves, and not to foreign captives who were owned by Jews. Mosaic laws declared the terms upon which a Hebrew, who had been sold, could redeem himself, or be redeemed by his friends; and his right to take with him his wife and children, when discharged from bondage.

The main point of this reference is that the slaves of the ancient world were considered with some humanity. This was none the less true of ancient Asia and Africa. In fact, in Africa, in both ancient and modern times, slaves have been known to rise above their servitude and become kings in the very houses in which they had been slaves.

The fact that slavery existed in West Africa prior to contact with Europeans is often used to excuse the European slave trade. The two systems had few similarities. The tragic and distinguishing feature of the slave trade that was introduced by the European was that it totally dehumanized the slave. This dehumanization continued in many ways throughout the slavery period and well into the colonial era. This crucial act was supported by a rationale that was created, in part, by the Christian Church and later extended by the writers of the seventeenth and eighteenth century. The myth of a people with no history and culture comes out of this period. All myths are contagious and one can create many others. This fact can be better understood after some insight into how and why the slave trade came to be.

Early in the fifteenth century, Europe began to recover from the wounds of the Middle Ages and the Crusades. European skill in shipbuilding had improved and, in search of a food supply for their hungry population and for new worlds to conquer, Europeans began to venture beyond their shores. There are many reasons why the Europeans had not embarked upon worldwide exploration before this time: their ships were small and unsafe for long sea journeys; oars were sometimes used to propel these ships and the outcome of all voyages depended largely on the wind; there were no good maps or instruments to guide sailors through unknown waters.

At that time most Europeans were ignorant about the shape of the world and some of them thought it was flat. The Portuguese set out to disprove this and, about the middle of the fifteenth century, they began trading with the people along the west coast of Africa, to which they gave the name "guinea" after the Sudanic Empire of Ghana. At first they traded mainly in gold, but before long they began to take slaves also.

Social and political unrest began to develop among some of the nations of West Africa at the time Europe was regaining its strength and a degree of

unity.   The first Europeans to visit the west coast
of Africa did not have to fight their way in — they
came as guests and were treated as guests.   Later,
they decided to stay as conquerors and slave
traders.   In order to gain a position strong enough
to attain these ambitions, they began to take sides
in African family disputes, very often supplying
the family or tribe they favored with arms and using
their   favorites   as   slave catchers.   A number of
African nations went into the slave trade in order
to buy guns and other European manufactured items.
Others were forced to capture slaves or become
slaves.

The Europeans did not come to Africa initially to
find slaves.   For years they had been hearing
stories about the great riches of Africa.   At the
Battle of Ceuta against the Moslems in 1415, Prince
Henry of Portugal, who later became known as
Prince Henry the Navigator, heard about the pros-
perity of Timbuktu and the wealth of the great
states along the west coast of Africa.   He also
heard stories about a great African Christian king
named Prester John.

Before the end of the fifteenth century, the
Portuguese sailors had come to know the general
shape of the continent of Africa.   They traded
regularly with African countries from 1471 on.
Forts were built along the coast of West Africa.
The most famous of these forts, still in existence,
is Elmina Castle in what is now Ghana.   This fort
was started in 1482 by a Portuguese captain, Don
Diego d'Azambuja.   Because of the large profits
gained by the Portuguese in their trading in this
country,   they called it the Gold Coast.

During the latter half of the fifteenth century,
European nationalism was reflected in the expansion
of trade in both slaves and manufactured goods.
The marriage of Queen Isabella and King Ferdinand
gave Europe the unity to drive out the Arabs and the
Moors.   Both Spain and Portugal were becoming
powerful Mediterranean nations.

In 1488,   Bartholomew Diaz had sailed around the
southern tip of Africa.   About ten years later,
another Portuguese sailor,   Vasco da Gama,   sailed

past the point reached by Diaz. With the help of an Arab pilot, Vasco da Gama reached India in 1498. For Europe, the door to the vast world of Asia was open.

The rationale for justifying the slave trade had already started in Europe with Europeans attempting to justify the enslavement of other Europeans. This is a neglected aspect of history that is rarely taken into consideration. There was a concerted effort to obtain European labor to open up the vast regions of the New World. In what became the United States, White enslavement started before Black enslavement. In an article, "White Servitude in the United States," published in *Ebony* in November 1969, the Afro-American historian Lerone Bennett, Jr., gives the following information about this period:

> When someone removes the cataracts of whiteness from our eyes, and when we look with unclouded vision on the bloody shadows of the American past, we will recognize for the first time that the Afro-American, who was so often second in freedom, was also second in slavery.
> Indeed, it will be revealed that the Afro-American was third in slavery. For he inherited his chains, in a manner of speaking, from the pioneer bondsmen, who were red and white.

The enslavement of both red men and white men in the early American colonies was a contradiction of English law. The colonies were founded with the understanding that neither chattel slavery nor villeinage would be recognized. Yet forced labor was widely used in England. This system was transferred to the colonies and used to justify a form of slavery that was visited upon red and white men. Concise information on this system and how it developed is revealed in the book, *Slavery and Abolition, 1831-1841*, by Albert Bushnell Hart, first published in 1906.

It was decreed that the apprentice must serve his seven years, and take floggings as his master saw fit; the hired servant must carry out his contract for his term of service. Convicts of the state, often including political offenders, were slaves of the state and were sometimes sold to private owners overseas. The colonists claimed those rights over some of their white fellow countrymen. There was a large class of "redemptioners" who had agreed that their service should be sold for a brief term of years to pay their passage-money, and of "indentured" or "indented" servants, brought by their masters under legal obligation, who served even longer terms, subject to the same penalties of branding, whipping, and mutilation as African slaves. These forms of servitude were supposed to be limited in duration and transmitted no claim to the servant's children. In spite of this servitude, the presumption, in law, was that a white man was born free.

The English settlers had, at once, begun to enslave their Indian neighbors, soothing their consciences with the argument that it was right to make slaves of pagans. In large numbers, the Indians fled or died in captivity, leaving few of their descendants in bondage. The virgin soil of the new English settlements continued to need more labor. This led to a fierce search for white labor that subsequently led to a search for black labor.

Bennett continues: "It has been estimated that at least two out of every three white colonists worked for a term of years in the fields or kitchens as semi-slaves...white servitude was the historic foundation upon which the system of black slavery was constructed."

There is a need to examine the slave trade and slavery with fresh insight and with a focus on long neglected aspects of this subject. Africans played a major role in opening up the New World for European settlement. Their labor and the raw material taken from their countries were important features in the development of the European Industrial Revolution.

Professors Lloyd Best, Edgar A. Toppin, Staughton Lynd and Sterling Stuckey have shown how slavery developed as an institution along with the plantation system where the Africans were transformed into a people that were later referred to as

Negroes. In most cases every attempt was made to destroy their African culture, their language, and everything that they remembered from the time before they were slaves. These writers have asked questions that cannot be put aside without clear and honest answers. These questions and these answers are intended to open up a new study of the slave trade and slavery in particular and early American history in general.

John Henrik Clarke
January 1970

PART I: FACTS & FUNDAMENTALS:

INITIAL LESSONS IN SLAVERY AND THE AFRICAN SLAVETRADE

COMMENTARY

John Henrik Clarke

The discovery of Africa by the Europeans was a fortunate incident in the history of the European and a most tragic incident in the history of the African. The Africans who came in contact with the European had no clear understanding of the European mind then and has no clear understanding of the European mind now. These two peoples met at the crossroads of history at a time when they could have complemented each other; they could have changed the world by forming a partnership. Instead one chose to subdue the other and traffic them as slaves. The results of this decision reverberates throughout the world until this day.

Between 1400 and 1600, a major decision was made in Europe, among Europeans, without being announced to the rest of the world. The decision was made that the world would be mainly European dominated, politically, economically and culturally. This decision was made despite the fact that Europe and the Europeans were just emerging from what they called their Middle Ages, from the aftermath of the Crusades which was a drain on their economy, and from famine and plagues that were a drain on their population. The main unifying factor in Europe at that time was a uniquely organized political organization, better known as the Catholic Church. Without its sanction, at least in part, the Europeans would not have gone into the African slave trade.

The Arab slave trade in North and in East Africa had been a well-established institution long before the Arabs accepted Islam. With the rise of Islam in the seventh century, they used this new religion as further justification for their involvement in the slave trade. Islam, like Christianity, declared war on all forms of African religion and culture and later denied that Africans had anything worthy of being called a religion or a culture. The Africans were totally unprepared to deal with this kind of mentality at the time of its initial emergence; they are totally unprepared to deal with it now.

Eric Williams starts his book, *Capitalism and Slavery*, with the following information that reflects the temper and temperament of this period in history. He says:

When in 1492 Columbus, representing the Spanish monarchy, discovered the New World, he set in train the long and bitter international rivalry over colonial possessions for which, after four and a half centuries, no solution has yet been found. Portugal, which had initiated the movement of international expansion, claimed the new territories on the ground that they fell within the scope of a papal bull of 1455 authorizing her to reduce to servitude all infidel peoples. The two powers, to avoid controversy, sought arbitration and, as Catholics, turned to the Pope — a natural and logical step in an age when the universal claims of the Papacy were still unchallenged by individuals and governments. After carefully sifting the rival claims, the Pope issued in 1493 a series of papal bulls which established a line of demarcation between the colonial possessions of the two states: the East went to Portugal and the West went to Spain. The partition, however, failed to satisfy Portuguese aspirations and in the subsequent year the contending parties reached a more satisfactory compromise in the Treaty of Tordesillas, which rectified the papal judgement to permit Portuguese ownership of Brazil.

The above accounting reflects the extreme arrogance of the Europeans of that day in assuming that they could arbitrarily take what did not belong to them and make decisions about the lives of millions of people without consulting a single one of them. This arrogance has not changed to this day irrespective of the European religion and politics, or the lack of it. This is the essence of world-wide racism.

Dr. A. Adu Boahen's article, "The Coming of the Europeans," in the book, *The Horizon History of Africa*, is a good summary of the impact of the European coming to the west coast of Africa and the establishment of the West African slave trade. Europe was unable to mount a unified action of this nature prior to this date because of the late emergence of the nation-state as a factor in the politics of Europe. Prior to this time Europeans had been mainly at war with each other over territory, sometimes for religious reasons and other times for reasons that made no sense to anyone except themselves. This was tribal warfare in its truest sense, although Europeans are reluctant to admit it. Once Europeans partly settled the internal disputes among themselves they found they had enough unity to turn on other people.

When the Europeans started looking outside of Europe for ways to satisfy their needs, they were not looking for Africa. They were searching for trade routes to the sweets and spices of Asia. They stopped in Africa looking for the legendary Christian African King, Prestor John, in the hopes of soliciting his help in their fight against what they called the infidel Arabs. It must be remembered that while they called the Arabs infidels, the Arabs also referred to them as infidels.

A lot of maritime information coming out of China, then the leading maritime nation of the world, had been preserved by the Africans and the

3

Arabs who had been militarily and intellectually in control of Spain and parts of the Iberian Peninsula since 711 A.D. What the Europeans learned from this maritime information renewed their interest in shipbuilding and the skills of the sea again. This information was put to good use by Prince Henry of Portugal, known in history as Henry the Navigator. He opened schools in Portugal where Europeans learned the basics of seafaring skills and were re-introduced to the concept of longitude and and latitude. The talk about the shape of the world, whether it was round or flat, was part of the folklore and mythology of that time. Round or flat was not settled in the European mind during that period. What was settled was that whatever the shape, round or flat, they wanted to control all of it. The years between 1400 and 1600 were a major turning point in human history. At the end of this period the world would have changed again in such a way that it would never be the same again.

African and Asian labor, resources and energy helped Europe lay the basis for the modern scientific and technical world. The tyranny of technology, propaganda, forced religion, and forced labor, all functioned together to assist in the European take-over of most of the world. Their greatest achievement being in the area of propaganda, in essence, the conquest of the mind. They colonized religious literature, they colonized religious images to make them more favorable to themselves, but the most disastrous of all their colonizations was the colonization of the image of god. In most of Africa influenced by the Christian Europeans and the Islamic Arabs, Africans were looked on with contempt if they dared envision a god looking like themselves. And through missionary and Islamic training many Africans began to strive to be those things most unlike themselves. A great Caribbean scholar of the nineteenth century, Edward W. Blyden, said:

In all English speaking countries the mind of the intelligent Negro child revolts against the description of the Negro given in elementary books —

4

geographies, travels, histories ....

Having embraced or at least assented to these falsehoods about himself, he concludes that his only hope of rising in the scale of respectable manhood is to strive for whatever is most unlike himself and most alien to his peculiar tastes. And whatever his literary attainments or acquired ability, he fancies that he must grind at the mill which is provided for him, putting in material furnished to his hands, bringing no contribution from his own field; and of course nothing comes out but what is put in.

I would be happy to say that after slavery and the effects of its aftermath we are out of this dilemma of self-identity and misguided direction. However, quite the contrary is true. We seem to be in the same dilemma now, more tragically and deeper than ever. This is why it is necessary to examine this period in history to see where we went wrong and why we paid so much and for so long for a crime we did not commit. If the present and the past is always an extension of the same thing then the future cannot be successfully planned without an understanding of both. This is why I repeatedly look back at the fifteenth and sixteenth centuries in order to understand the twentieth with the hope of projecting for the twenty-first.

Africa has always been the prize of the nations that discovered and beheld its potential and its possibilities. Africa has always had and still has things that other people want, cannot do without, and don't want to pay for. Most people who lust after Africa and its richness know more about Africa's potential than many Africans themselves. This is why the European in the fifteenth and sixteenth centuries was willing to establish an honorable commodity trade with the people of Asia while setting up a trade dealing with the trafficking of human beings in Africa. Such commodity trading that was done in Africa was the dumping of rum, bric-a-brac, cheaply made fabrics, and trinkets, the experimental objects coming out of the embryo of what would later become the European industrial revolution. Without the resources and the labor of African people, this revolution would

5

not have occurred at all.

It is my estimation that the British late entry into the slave trade gave this unfortunate business order and focus. The British had settled or decided they did not have to settle the dispute with the Catholic Church. They no longer felt obligated to go to the church to get permission to engage in the expanding and lucrative business of the slave trade in Africa. They sailed up the river, marked off ten miles on each side and arbitrarily called the area Gambia. This territory was a part of the Sene-Gambia and by this act the British began the partitioning of Africa, irrespective of previous borders or cultures. This partitioning would not end until the Berlin Conference of 1884-1885 which created most of the artificial African nation-states of today. These political nation-states, as designed by the Europeans, are about as un-African as anything can be. Traditionally, all the great states of Africa's golden ages were multi-ethnic and multicultural territorial states. The nation-states as designed by the Europeans put Africans in a political strait-jacket — it retards the growth and imagination of African people. On this point see Basil Davidson's book, *The Black Man's Burden: The Curse of the Nation-State.*

The age of exploration in Africa was also the age of learning for the Europeans. At first they had a favorable attitude toward the Africans and recorded this favorable attitude in their many chronicles and diaries. They spoke highly of African political institutions and their sophistication; and from their own records, on more than one occasion, they state that the Africans were civilized to the marrow of their bones. When they needed a rationale to start their trafficking in human cargo, they changed their minds about the Africans and invented the African as a savage.

Concurrent with the spread of slavery in West Africa the monastic order or the order of the monks was spreading in North Africa. North Africa was not removed from the slave trade — slavery was already an established fact there before the West

6

African slave trade. The slave trade in North Africa and in the Mediterranean area was no respecter of color or nationality. The capture of white people in the Mediterranean area was extensive and often they were held for ransom until some European country paid for their release.

After the Arabs lost their power in Spain and in the Iberian Peninsula some of the Arabs enslaved the Africans who had previously been the military arm of their staying power in the area. The first Africans to be brought to the New World did not come directly from the coast of West Africa; they came from Spain and the Iberian Peninsula. Many of these Africans were not raw, untrained labor; they included explorers, adventurers, freebooters, and skilled craftsmen.

In the meantime, the great drama and ordeal of slavery was unfolding in the forts, castles, and slave-holding stations along the coast of West Africa. Because of the gun and of the cooperation of some corrupt Africans, Europeans were now able to penetrate into the hinterlands for a new supply of slaves. Demand for slaves had increased world-wide and so did the ruthlessness of the catching practices, the maintenance in the holding stations, and the transfer of slaves across the Atlantic. The British had brought some order to the competition between slave-traders. There were now respected spheres of influence. Arguments and competition between European slave-traders were held to a minimum in order to extract the maximum profit from this dirty business.

The conditions in the dungeons and holding stations along the coast of West Africa were a hell beyond imagination. Slaves were assembled in these dungeons until buyers and ships arrived. The massive bastardization of African people by the forced violation of the African woman began in these holding stations. The African woman had no choice but to submit to the slave-trader's will and the African man had no means of protecting her. This condition would continue on the slave-ships, on the plantations of the New World and, to some extent, years after slavery was abolished; and it is not

7

totally absent today.

In what is referred to as the New World, the Africans continued their resistance to slavery which started with their capture in the homeland. In the New World they used different methods, depending on their circumstances. In South America and on many islands in the Caribbean, the slave population outnumbered the European and was difficult to maintain. Many newly arriving Africans by-passed the auction block, fled into the hinterlands and formed separate African communities. In Brazil they formed two African states, Bahia and Palmyres.

The slave-masters in the Caribbean Islands and in South America generally bought slaves in large lots and kept the lots together. They thought they could work them better that way. They were right. There was one aspect they did not take into consideration — they could also revolt better that way. These slaves came from the same general area in Africa. They had the same basic culture, language, and belief system and this was the basis of the cultural continuity which enabled them to organize and maintain the most successful slave revolts in the so-called New World.

In the United States the business of slave buying and selling operated similar to a brokerage system. If a trader bought ten slaves early in the week, he might sell five or more of them by the end of the week. In breaking them up often and sending them in different directions, cultures, languages, and customs were being broken up. In essence, cultural continuity and, worst of all, the African family structure were being systematically destroyed.

The Africans played many cultural and dramatic roles in the making of the Americas other than that of slave. Their presence changed two hemispheres and the world of their day. Their labor given against their will recharged the economy of Europe and gave birth to what would become the modern day scientific, technical, and capitalistic world. Their resistance to the slave conditions in the Caribbean and in the Americas put on record some of the most dramatic slave revolts in human history. Although their culture and their religion was often outlawed, and because the slave population outnumbered the slave-masters', they influenced the culture of their slave-masters to the point where their slave-masters' culture became somewhat subservient to theirs.

In Brazil there was such a drastic shortage of European women that Portuguese men received permission from the Catholic Church to marry African women. Some of the first families of Brazil were born of these marriages. It is often forgotten that for the first one hundred-fifty years of New World exploration very few white women were brought to the New World. The marriages between these two groups did not change the nature of slavery. Slavery was fierce and brutal and so was the organized resistance to it.

Within a very few generations the majority of the people referred to as Indians were either extinct or had their lives so disrupted that their way of life would never be the same. I am referring to large settlements of people which covered the land masses of North America, South America and the islands of the Caribbean — millions of people with their own cultures and ways of life. Many did not resist the European because they did not think they had to. They assumed that the European came in friendship as had all of the other people they had encountered in their long history on this earth.

For the next three hundred years slavery and its aftermath was the most profitable enterprise in the world. It had disrupted the cultures of most of the world and had become a three continent trade connection. This enterprise set several revolutions in motion that still affect our lives today. There was a revolution in shipbuilding and maritime enterprise. There was a revolution in trade and commerce. There was a revolution in social thought. The rationalization and the explanation for slavery made some men mortgage the morality of their souls in order to live with themselves. Some Christians claimed they were attempting to save the heathen soul of the African;

9

others said the African had no soul and was not even
seen as a step-child in the eyes of god. Some of
the abolitionists were paternalistic and conde-
scending in their attitudes toward the African.
Some boldly admitted that they could accept the
African as a freedman but could never accept the
African as a brother. This contradiction continued
until the British abolitionists called for the
elimination of traffic in slaves by the sea.

A bootleg slave trade and slave smuggling would
continue for another one hundred years in an
atmosphere of slave resistance and slave revolts.
The resistance to slavery which had started on the
shores of Africa continued on the slave ships and
extended beyond the auction block. In his book,
Forced Migration, Dr. Joseph E. Inikore described
the background and the development of this
situation. Father Bartoleme de Las Casas in his
book, *The Devastation of the Indies,* describes the
destruction of the indigenous population of the
Caribbean Islands that created the necessity for an
increase in the Atlantic slave trade in order to
replace the so-called Indians as a labor supply.
The Africans were brought to the New World mainly as
a labor supply to maintain the lucrative profits
made in the slave trade by the establishment of the
plantation systems. This labor supply was forced
beyond human endurance, thereby setting slave
revolts in motion.

Another process was set in motion on the shores
of Africa that continued on the slave ships and in
the New World. This process is generally left out
of history and commentary on slavery because it
deals with the morality of the Europeans involved in
the slave trade and belies the claim that Europeans
were trying to bring the Africans under the
protection of Christianity. This process was the
extensive rape and physical violation of the African
woman. The aftermath is reflected in the fact that
today over half of the Africans who live outside of
Africa have some degree of European blood in their
veins. On the plantations in the Caribbean
Islands, South America and the United States many
white males had their first sexual experience with

an African slave woman.   She was not in a position
to say no or resist them exercising their lust.
This was lust that had no resemblance to love.   The
African man could not protect her because he also
was a slave.   This is one of the unacknowledged
tragedies of the slavery system and, in my opinion,
one of the greatest tragedies in history.   I have
previously said that there is no way to go directly
into this subject and be understood.   Western
historians and "authorities" on the cultures of
peoples and societies have not,   in most cases,
accorded the African people a place in their
respectful commentaries.   They have been sparing
and often totally reluctant to use the words
"history" and "culture" in matters relating to
African people.   In approaching this subject it is
necessary, at least briefly, to establish the fact
that African culture is not only a part of world
culture, but may well be the basis of world
culture.   It was this culture that sustained the
Africans during the holocaust of the slave trade and
the colonial system that followed it.   In South and
Central America and in the Caribbean Islands,
African culture,   reborn on alien soil, became the
cohesive force and the communication system that
helped to set in motion some of the most successful
slave revolts in history.
     On the same subject I have further stated that,
in many ways, the plantations were small, semi-auto-
nomous states. The plantation owners and their overseers had complete authority over the lives of the
Africans.   Very often their attempt to break the
spirit of the Africans set the thought pattern of
revolt in motion.   The newly arrived Africans were
the most effective in the early slave revolts.
They were closer to the African culture and had not
adjusted to this new way of life.   These Africans
and Europeans were part of a world drama,   the most
massive movement of people in human history.   The
writer,   Frank Tannenbaum,   described the event in
this manner:

11

The settling of the Western Hemisphere by people
coming from Europe and Africa was an adventure on a
grand scale, involving diverse people, cultures,
millions of human beings, and hundreds of years.
The common element was the New World, though
strangely dissimilar in physical features and
cultural types. But the student discerns many an
analogous design, patterned by the newcomers as
they established themselves in the strange and
unexplored regions.

This great drama of human movement had started in
Europe and its roots can be traced to the period of
the Crusades when Europeans became aware of the
broader world beyond their shores. Early in the
fifteenth century, Europe began to recover from the
wounds and conflicts of the Middle Ages. European
skill in shipbuilding had improved and they had
already created embryo technology, including the
gun.

Although the Europeans never declared it to be
so, they proved in many ways that the gun had been
elevated to the status of a deity. By their
actions they proved that the gun not only gave them
privilege over other people, it gave them rights
over the lives of other people. The Europeans'
position and their attitude did not stop the African
slave revolts. They still revolted in different
ways, in different places. The most sustained
revolts in the Caribbean Islands were in Jamaica and
in Haiti, the richest and the most productive of
the islands at the time.

In South America, the major slave revolts
occurred in Guyana, then under Dutch rule, and
Brazil, then under Portuguese rule. Slave revolts
in the United States were more numerous but less
successful because slaves in the United States did
not have access to the forests and the mountains
where they could secret themselves and survive
undetected. The best documentation of these
revolts is in Herbert Aptheker's *American Negro
Slave Revolts*.

I maintain that slavery and its consequences have
never been fully understood in this country and the
world, academically or otherwise. The African

12

people who were brought to the United States not only changed the character of the United States, they changed the character of the world, and they changed their own character in such a way that they could never again be the same as the African people who were taken out of Africa. They are, of course, still an African people, although mutilated, changed by time and circumstances and by conditions over which they had no control.

It must be understood that they were not brought to the English colonies to be given citizenship or to share in democracy. They were brought here for one and one reason alone, and that was as a cheap and hopefully inexhaustible labor supply. They were not expected to survive, but they did, and prevailed. Even today when most white Americans visualize an American citizen, black Americans are not a part of their vision. If this is a terrible contradiction, the presence of a large number of African people in the United States, a number more than equal to the population of five European nations, is an even greater contradiction. In this country African people constitute a nation within a nation who have been deprived of a recognized nationality. White people in the United States have never said, in an overt way, you are welcomed here. Africans in Africa have never said, in an overt way, you are welcomed to return home. The Africans in the United States are a national dilemma within a dilemma multiplied by an enigma. I think the following explanation given by Lerone Bennett, Jr. in his book, *The Challenge of Blackness*, is clearer and more precise than mine. He says:

> If black people are not what white people said they were, then white America is not what it claims to be. What we have to deal with here therefore is a contestation at the level of reality. We are engaged in a struggle over meaning, in a struggle over the truth. And it is my argument here that blacks and not whites embody the common interest and the truth of American society.

13

The aftermath of the slave trade might be worse than the trade itself mainly because the major participants in the trade have made a mission out of lying about their participation in this the greatest of all human tragedies. In the last twenty years the academic interpreters of the Atlantic slave trade have been pointing their fingers at the African participants, as though the trade could not have existed without them. Any honest researcher, familiar with the documents, knows that the role of the African was minor in comparison to that of the European and the Arab. The Atlantic slave trade was a three-continent industry that affected a revolution in shipping, in economics and in world trade. Africans did not have this kind of connection at this juncture in history; and, besides, the slave trade was mainly a European and an Arab business. I do not, in any way, intend to free Africans of any guilt for their participation in this trade — their involvement was tragic, misguided and not without significance, but the slave trade would have occurred whether the African participated or not.

Both Christianity and Islam were used to rationalize this trade. The Christian and the Moslem believed that their gods approved of what they were doing: their rationale being that they were doing this to heathens (or infidels) who were outside of the grace of god.

I have always maintained that all history is a current event. Everything that has ever happened continues to happen. And slavery will be with us until we eliminate it within ourselves. To begin to eliminate it within ourselves, we must begin by being honest about it. It did occur, hundred-plus millions of people did die, and multi-millions of people did suffer enslavement without any compensation for their labor and without any apologies for the crimes that were committed against them. This is not an issue that will go away soon — it is not like the rain that will go away and come again another day. African people, European people, and Arab people must face up to their participation in this trade, frontally. However, all of them share some degree of responsibility.

Millions of people live better material lives today because of the slave trade, some corrupt Africans included; still, in a collective way, African people were the major losers. Both the winners and the losers must confront the reality of their role in this tragedy. But before they can confront the world, they first must confront themselves because they can change the world if first they change themselves.

THE SLAVE TRADE

John Henrik Clarke

To understand the African slave trade, we must understand slavery as an institution — an institution almost as old as human society. Every people, some time or another, have been slaves. In fact, Europeans enslaved other Europeans for a much longer period than they enslaved Africans. Slavery was a permanent feature of the ancient world, in Egypt, Kush, and Rome.

The African slave period is best known to us because it is the best-documented. However, these documents are often confusing because they were created by people who were trying to justify the slave trade. Most people, especially Europeans who created most of the documents on the slave trade, write about the subject with the intent to make the victim of slavery feel guilty and to vindicate the perpetrators of the slave trade.

There is probably more dishonesty related to the interpretation of this subject than any other subject known to man. The African slave trade, like African history, is often written about but rarely understood. This misunderstanding probably grows out of the fact that we nearly always start the study of the African slave trade in the wrong place. The germ, the motive, the rationale for the African slave trade started in the minds of the Europeans in the fifteenth and the sixteenth centuries. The slave trade could not have started at all had there been no market for it. The slave trade started when the Europeans began to expand out into the broader world; the market was created by Europeans for European reasons.

The story of the African slave trade is

essentially the story of the consequences of the
second rise of Europe. In the years between the
passing of the Roman Empire in the eighth
century and the partial unification of Europe
through the framework of the Catholic church in the
fifteenth century, Europeans were engaged mainly in
internal matters. With the opening of the New
World and the expulsion of the Arabs and the Moors
from Spain during the latter part of the fifteenth
century, the Europeans started to expand beyond
their homeland into the broader world. They were
searching for new markets, new materials, new manpower, and new land to exploit. The African slave
trade was created to accommodate this expansion.
The basis for the European industrial revolution
had already been established. They had already
created embryo technology, including the gun. In
the years that followed, they also used other
advantages, mainly a large fleet of ships and
rabble soldiers and sailors with no sentimental
attachment to non-European people, to take over
most of the world. In so doing, they destroyed a
large number of nations and civilizations that were
older than any in Europe.
The main problem with the African, in dealing
with the European during this early period, was the
African's tragic naivete. He had never dealt
extensively with this kind of people. He came out
of a society where nature was kind; nature
furnished him enough food, enough land, enough of
the basic things he needed to live a pretty good
life. These old African societies were governed by
honor and obligation. Land could neither be bought
or sold; there were no fights over ownership of
land. The land belonged to everyone.
The European, coming from a society where nature
was rather stingy and where he had to compete with
his brother for his breakfast, his land, and his
woman, had acquired a competitive nature that the
African could not deal with. In order to justify
the destruction of these African societies, a
monster that still haunts our lives was created.
This monster was racism. The slave trade and the
colonial system that followed are the parents of

"Slave Traffic on the Coast of Africa," a painting by A. F. Biards, depicts some of the base elements involved in the villainous barter and enslavement of human beings from the continent of Africa.   (*Hull Museums*)

this catastrophe. The Europeans, mainly the Portuguese, who came to the west coast of Africa in the fifteenth century, were not at first looking for slaves. The search for gold and other treasures lured them to Africa. They did not have to fight their way into the continent; they came as guests and were treated as guests. Then they grew strong, decided to be conquerors, and turned on their hosts.

Another myth we have to dispel is that the Europeans came to Africa to spread civilization. Actually, most of the great civilizations in Africa declined after the coming of the Europeans. For years the Europeans had been hearing rumors about African cities of gold and beautiful women.

There were also legends circulated in Europe about a great emperor in Ethiopia called Prester John. But when the Portuguese arrived in Africa, Prester John had been dead for three hundred years; and they looked for him on one side of Africa, and he had been on the other. But no European came to Africa to tame any raw savage. When the Europeans

19

first saw the cities of Africa, they reported that these cities were well designed, and that the African was civilized to the marrow of his bones.

Fifty years later, when they wanted to justify the slave trade, they started the myths about savage Africa, with no organized societies, no cities, even no knowledge of the wheel. The European did not enter Africa to bring civilization. In fact, no nation ever invaded another nation for any reason other than to exploit that nation for its own reasons. This is true even when Whites invade Whites. It's true when Browns invade Browns. And it's also true when Blacks invade Blacks. The intent of every invader, no matter what his color, is to establish his own way of life; and, in nearly every case, the local culture suffers.

This happened when the Europeans invaded the west coast of Africa. We have their word that they did not meet any uncivilized people. We also have their word that they encountered not only well-organized societies but societies that had a great deal of order and beauty.

In 1434, a small fleet of Portuguese ships sailed down the coast of Africa and established some trading posts. By 1441, they were taking some of the tropical riches out of Africa and also a few slaves they bought who had been prisoners of war captured in some local skirmishes among Africans. By 1482, they had built the fortress of Elmina Castle, the beginning of forts built by Europeans along the coast of West Africa to protect themselves from the Africans when the slave trade was established. In fact, the slave trade did not really get under way until the Europeans had these

The midwestern coast of Africa was soon turned into an assortment of castles and forts such as this English fort: the Cape Coast Castle. (*National Maritime Museum*)

fortresses built. And while building the forts, with the help of Africans, they were telling the Africans that they had come to deal in honorable trade; and the naive Africans believed this story. These fortresses actually served as holding stations for the slaves that they were shipping to the New World. Incidentally, the Scandinavians entered the slave trade after the Portuguese; but they did not have any appreciable success, and they became middlemen in the slave trade.

Then, when the Arabs and the Moors were expelled from Spain, they returned to Africa — after being masters of the Mediterranean for 750 years. They had no sentimental attachment to Africa. They began to prey on the nations south of the Sahara, principally the old empire of Songhai. They first claimed the salt mines, for salt was then so precious that traders gave two parts of gold for one part of salt. They sent troops from what is now Morocco down into this area. The fight over the salt mines at Taghaza on the edge of the Sahara Desert became a great political and economic struggle.

But something else happened, too. Christopher Columbus had, by sheer accident, started out to look for the East Indies and instead found what was later called the West Indies. A new world was opened to Europeans, and they promptly began their exploitation.

After Columbus tried and failed to make good use of Indian labor, he introduced the idea of using

The forts and castles were used as residences for European slavers and as slave dens for Africans who would have to await shipment to their various destinations. (*Photograph by John R. Freeman*)

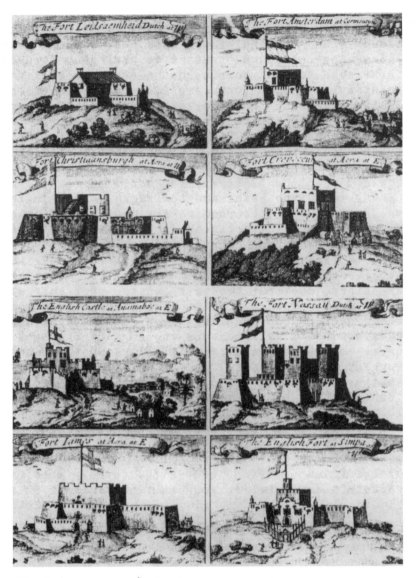

The Portuguese were the first to indulge in the slave trade and were soon followed by the Dutch, Swedes, Danes, French, Germans, and English. *(Photograph by John R. Freeman)*

African slaves. He had visited the west coast of Africa before his voyage to the New World and noted the internal disputes between African nations. He introduced to Europe the idea of using African labor in the New World.

In the meantime, Portugal and Spain, having broken part of the Moorish power in the Mediterranean, began to vie for spheres of influence. As good Catholic nations, they went to the Pope to settle a dispute; and the Pope told them, in essence, you take the east and you take the west. Spain began to gravitate toward the west and Portugal toward the east. Using maps made by Jews who dealt in gold in northern and western Africa, a Portuguese prince called Henry the Navigator who, incidentally, never went to sea, began to send Portuguese expeditions down the coast of West Africa, first for trade, then to establish Portuguese holdings in that area.

When the Moors were expelled from Spain, they returned to Morocco, where the emperor El Mansur arranged with them to invade Equatorial Africa, the old empire of Songhai. This invasion broke up the structure of the last great empire in Western Africa. And the chaos that followed set up Africa for the future European slave trade.

Sir John Hawkins led the British into the slave trade and made the slave trade big business. He gave it a system of organization, establishing spheres of influence and agreements among slave traders that one would not infringe on the territory of another. Christianity played a major role in

Those who established and engaged themselves in the newly lucrative enterprise reduced the African to slavery through violent repressive acts. Branding was one of them and served as a means of identifying one's property. This particular set of brands belonged to George Hyde Clarke, who operated large plantations in Jamaica. (*Hull Museums*)

setting up the rationale for the African slave trade, and no slave trader used Christianity more extensively than Captain Hawkins.

In the meantime, the Portuguese were driven out of their holdings in West Africa. They transferred their slave trading from the inner coast down to the Congo and, later on, further down into the small kingdom of Matamba, which was later called Angola. Later, the Portuguese went down the southward coast of Africa and established themselves in the city of Luanda, which was built by Africans before the coming of the Europeans and was a modern city in every respect.

The Portuguese continued around to East Africa and established themselves at the kingdom of Monomatapa, named after the king who ruled over a Southeast African country that the Africans now called Zimbabwe. There was no difficulty in converting this king to Christianity because there was no conflict between the preachment of Christianity and what already existed in African religion.

The slave trade prospered, and the Africans continued to be poured into the New World. Figures on the subject vary, but it has been estimated that during the years of the African slave trade, Africa lost from 60 to 100 million people. This was the greatest single crime ever committed against a people in world history. It was also the most tragic act of protracted genocide.

Exercises

Questions for Discussion

1. Did Slavery exist as an institution before the beginning of the African slave trade? If so, can you name some periods during which it existed and some of the peoples among whom it existed?

2. How did the African slave trade get started? What kept it alive?

3. Why is the African slave period the best known to us of all the periods of institutional slavery?

4. Why do we refer to African slave trade as a trade?

5. How did Europeans justify the enslavement of Africans? Was the justification made prior to the beginning of the slave trade or after it?

6. In what manner did the Portuguese establish themselves on the west coast of Africa? What were their early relations with the Africans there?

7. What circumstances in late fifteenth century Europe led ultimately to the intensification of the African slave trade?

8. Which European nations were most prominent in European expansion overseas in the late fifteenth and early sixteenth centuries? In which geographical areas did these nations, for the most part, establish their spheres of influence? How was the determination of such spheres of influence effected?

9. What events inside Africa itself made her vulnerable to the slave trade? Approximately how many people were taken from Africa during the years of the African slave trade?

10. Describe the role of Sir John Hawkins in the slave trade.

Activities

1. Consult a number of history books dealing with European history. Look through those sections dealing with the African slave trade of the seventeenth and eighteenth centuries. In each case, how does the author explain the emergence of the trade? (Note particularly his opening remarks on the subject.)

2. In the history books which you have consulted, is there any attempt to make a character study of the men who dealt in slavery, such as John Hawkins, or any detailed description of their methods? Are there any illustrations showing ships' holds or the conditions under which slaves were bartered and transported?

3. Consult several books dealing with the culture and everyday life during classical antiquity. Can you find any description of social stratification and, specifically, of slavery in Rome? Describe, on the basis of the information you have located, a normal day in the life of a Roman slave.

4. Look up the term "slavery" in as many reference works as you have access to (unabridged dictionaries, encyclopedias, specialized encyclopedias, that is, of history, of social sciences). Compare the definitions. How extensive are they? Do they deal specifically with any particular historical periods or forms of slavery? How many examples of slavery are given? Do all the books tend to repeat the same examples?

5. Can you find any information on the institution of slavery in Africa before the advent of the slave trade with Europeans? Compare the domestic system with that arising as a result of the slave trade. (Consult the bibliographies included in this book for leads.)

Suggested Readings

A History of West Africa to the Nineteenth Century. By Basil Davidson. Doubleday, Anchor Book, New York, 1966. See chapters 23 and 24, pp. 289–298.

Topics in West African History. By A. Abu Boahen. New York and London, 1964. See Section 111: "Europe in West Africa," pp. 103–127.

Capitalism and Slavery. By Eric Williams. Capricorn, New York, 1966. Chapters one and two are especially good on how the slave trade began, pp. 3–50.

Slave and Citizen: The Negro in the Americas. By Frank Tannenbaum. Vintage Book, Random House, New York, 1946. A good and straightforward short history of the Africans in the Americas.

Slavery in the Americas. By Herbert S. Klein. The University of Chicago Press, Chicago, Illinois, 1967. See parts one and two, pp. 1–57.

THE SLAVE TRADE
IN THE NEW WORLD

John Henrik Clarke

The Africans were no strangers to the New World; they seem to have been in North America and South America long before the appearance of slavery. The African features so evident on the Olmec statues in Mexico and South America indicate that African people were in the Americas hundreds of years before Columbus. This is more than an assumption, thanks to the research of Professor Leo Weiner, reported in his *Africa and the Discovery of America,* and the work of Harold G. Lawrence in another book called, *African Explorers to the New World.*

The first Africans who came to the New World were not in bondage, contrary to popular belief. Africans participated in some of the early expeditions, mainly with Spanish explorers. The best-known of these African explorers was Estevanico, sometimes known as Little Steven, who accompanied the de Vaca expedition during six years of wandering from Florida to Mexico. The remarkable thing about Estevanico, who came to America in 1527, is that he was a remarkable linguist. He learned the language of the Indians in a matter of weeks. Because of his knowledge of herbs and medicines, he was accepted as a deity by some Indian tribes.

In 1539, Estevanico set out from Mexico in a party with Fray Marcos de Niza in search of the fabulous Seven Cities of Cibola. When most of the expedition, including Fray Marcos, became ill, Estevanico went on alone and opened up what is now known as New Mexico and Arizona.

A number of historians have stated that Pedro Nino, one of the pilots of the command ship of

Christopher Columbus, was an African. In the
discovery of the Pacific in 1513, Balboa carried
thirty Africans, who helped clear the road across
the isthmus between the two oceans. In the
conquest of Mexico, Cortez was accompanied by a
number of Africans. Incidentally, one was a
pioneer of wheat farming in the New World.

In the exploration of Guatemala, Chile, Peru,
and Venezuela, Africans arrived nearly a hundred
years before they reappeared as slaves in Jamestown,
Virginia, in 1619.

Thus, Africans were major contributors to the
making of the New World, and they did not come
culturally empty-handed. Many of the Africans
brought to the New World such skills as ironworking,
leatherworking, carpentry.

Before the breaking up of the social structure of
the West African states such as Ghana and Songhai,
and the internal strife that made the slave trade
possible, many Africans, especially West Africans,
lived in a society in which university life was
fairly common and scholars were held in reverence.

In that period in West African history, the
University of Sankore at Timbuktu was flourishing,
and its great chancellor, the last of the monumental scholars of West Africa, Ahmed Baba reigned
over that university. A great African scholar, he
wrote 47 books, each on a separate subject. He
received all of his education within Africa; in
fact, he did not leave the Western Sudan until he
was exiled to Morocco during the invasion in 1594.

My point is this: There existed in Africa
prior to the beginning of the slave trade a cultural
way of life that in many ways was equal, if not
superior, to many of the cultures then existing in
Europe. And the slave trade destroyed these
cultures and created a dilemma that the African has
not been able to extract himself from to this day.

There were, in the Africans' past, rulers who
extended kingdoms into empires, great armies that
subdued entire nations, generals who advanced the
technique of military science, scholars with wisdom
and foresight, and priests who told of gods that

During a smallpox plague in Charleston, Africans were held on board ship to keep them free from infection. Sick or diseased slaves did not yield a very good price. (*Library of Congress*)

TO BE SOLD on board the

Ship *Bance-Yland*, on tuesday the 6th of *May* next, at *Afhley-Ferry* a choice cargo of about 250 fine healthy

NEGROES,

just arrived from the Windward & Rice Coaft. —The utmoft care has already been taken, and fhall be continued, to keep them free from the leaft danger of being infected with the SMALL-POX, no boat having been on board, and all other communication with people from *Charles-Town* prevented.

Auftin, Laurens, & Appleby.

N. B. Full one Half of the above Negroes have had the SMALL-POX in their own Country.

were kind and strong. But with the bringing of the African to the New World, every effort was made to destroy his memory of having ever been part of a free and intelligent people.

The greatest destroyer of African culture, the greatest exploiter of the African, was the plantation system of the New World. The African was transformed into something called a Negro. He was demeaned. This is the thing that is uniquely tragic about the African slave system. Of all the slave systems in the world, no other dehumanized the slave more than that started by the Europeans in the fifteenth century. Using the church as a rationale, they began to set up myths that nearly always read the African out of human history, beginning with the classification of the African as a lesser being. The Catholic Church's justification for slavery was that the African was being brought under the guidance of Christendom and that he would eventually receive its blessings.

It was an all-too-frequent happening that members of one family would never again see or know each other, due to obdurate slave dealers and purchasers. (*Library of Congress*)

The rationale was that slavery was a blessing to the African. It was not.

There were several competing slave systems in the New World. In order to understand the effects of these various systems on the personality of the Africans, we have to look at each one individually. In Cuba and Haiti, often the Africans were a majority in the population. This is also true of certain portions of Brazil. Therefore the system operated differently in these areas, and, although it was still slavery, the African had some cultural mobility.

In South America and in the West Indies, the slave master did not outlaw the African drum, African ornamentations, African religion, or other things dear to the African, remembered from his former way of life. This permitted a form of cultural continuity among the slaves in the West Indies, Cuba, and South America that did not exist in the United States.

In the Portuguese area, in the West Indies,

Every African—man, woman and child—was subjected to the demeaning indignities of inspection. (*Courtesy Schomburg Collection*)

and often in South America, the plantation owner
would buy a shipload or half a shipload of slaves.
These slaves usually came from the same areas in
Africa, and they naturally spoke the same language
and had the same basic culture. Families, in the
main, were kept together. If a slave on an island
was sold to a plantation owner at the other end of
the island, he could still walk to see his
relatives. This made for a form of cultural
continuity among the slaves in South America, Cuba,
and Haiti that later made their revolts more
successful than revolts in the United States.

In the United States, in the fight to destroy
every element of culture of the slaves, the system
was cruel. No other system did so much to demean
the personality of the slave, to deny his personality, or to ruthlessly sell family members away
from each other. The American slave system
operated almost like the American brokerage system.
If a person bought twenty slaves at the beginning of
the week, and found himself short of cash at the
end of the week, he might, if the price was right,
sell ten. These ten might be resold within a few
days. The family, the most meaningful entity in
African life, was systematically and deliberately
destroyed. But in South America, the slave
managed to stay in his group and therefore preserved
some of his cultural continuity.

In spite of these drastic drawbacks, the
Africans in the Americas, including the United
States, made a meaningful contribution to the
preservation of the countries in which they were
slaves.

Another neglected aspect of the African in the
New World is the role of the African women.
Comparatively few white women were brought to the
New World during the first hundred years. Many
families of the New World originated from
cohabitation between the white slave master and the
African woman. Later, this same slave master,
especially in the United States, made and supported
laws forbidding his own child to have an education
or sit beside him on public transportation. In
Haiti, the African woman sometimes had kind of

semilegal status. In South America, especially in Brazil, sometimes the white slave master married the African woman and she became a free person. These free African women in South America began to maneuver their husbands in an attempt to lessen the harshness of the slave system. In the United States, however, there could be no such maneuver.

Haiti and Cuba, during this early period, were dominated by their "mother countries." Wars were started within these countries to liberate them from their European masters. Africans made a meaningful contribution toward the early liberation of Cuba, Haiti, and other areas of South America; they fought with Simon Bolivar for the freedom of South America, and fought valiantly to free Haiti from the domination of the French.

In the United States, especially in the American Revolution, the African slave often took the place of a white person, who decided that he did not want to fight, and fought with the promise that he would get his freedom afterward. Thousands of Africans fought in the American Revolution with this promise. And, a little-known incident in our history is that thousands of Africans fought with the British when the British made the same promise and the African believed them. Apparently it depended on who got to him first.

The African was a major contributor in the making of the New World; the economy of the New World rested largely on slave labor. For many years, one-third of the trade of the New World was with the small island of Santo Domingo, which later became Haiti. Haiti and the other Caribbean islands also influenced the economic system of Europe.

Slavery and the slave trade was the first inter-national investment in capital. It was the first large-scale investment that was inter-continental. Many Europeans invested in ships and in goods and services taken from these African countries and became independently wealthy.

But the slave revolts continued. By the end of the seventeenth century, the picture of slavery began to change drastically. Economic necessity, not racial prejudice, originally directed the African slave trade to the New World. As early as 1663, a group of slaves joined a group of white indentured servants in a revolt. Some slaves took the Christian version of the Bible literally and believed that God meant for them to be free men— slaves such as Gabriel Prosser in Virginia, who led a revolt of 40,000 slaves in 1800. In 1822 in Charleston, South Carolina, a carpenter, Denmark Vesey, planned one of the most extensive slave revolts on record, but he was betrayed and put to death with many of his followers. And in 1831, Nat Turner led the greatest slave revolt ever to occur in Virginia.

The slaves never accepted their condition passively. In his book, *American Negro Slave Revolts*, Dr. Herbert Aptheker records 250 slave revolts.

The African slave in the Americas, in addition to assisting in the freedom and the economy of these countries, made a major contribution to his own freedom.

In the story of the rise and fall of great African states, and subsequently the slave trade, we are trying to deal with something much bigger than history itself. We are trying to deal with an old situation and a new situation and trying to address ourselves to the current cry for Black history and Black power.

Our major point is this: The African people who became slaves in the United States have been many things in history, good and bad. They have ruled great nations and they have destroyed great nations. They are profoundly human. And they have played every role in the human drama, from saint to buffoon. Slavery does not represent the sum total of our history.

We are searching for a definition of our African heritage and attempting to determine what it means to a people emerging from bondage into the light of freedom, reentering the mainstream of world history as participants.

A good definition of heritage, or history, is: Heritage is something acquired or transmitted by a

34

predecessor. It is also called a "legacy," "tradition," and "birthright." But when we speak of our people, perhaps a new and better definition is in order.

In his book *Tom Tom*, John Vandercrook said, "A race is like a man. Until it uses its own talent, takes pride in its own history, and loves its own memories, it can never fulfill itself completely." Heritage, in essence, is how a people have used their talents to command the respect of other people. The ultimate purpose of our heritage and heritage teaching, is to show our people how, through identity and through respect for themselves, they can work to liberate themselves from the old ties of bondage. A person's relationship to his heritage, after all, is the same as the relationship of a child to its mother.

Exercises

Questions for Discussion

1. What evidence tends to support the assumption that Africans were in the Americas hundreds of years before Columbus?

2. In terms of the history of Africa and of Africans, what is the significance of the expedition of de Vaca? Of Columbus? Of Balboa? Of Cortez?

3. In what way did the slave system initiated by Europeans in the fifteenth and sixteenth centuries differ from prior slave systems?

4. What was the role of the Christianity in the development of the American slave system?

5. In what way or ways did the slave system in the West Indies and in South America differ from the slave system in the United States?

6. What was the status of the African woman during the first hundred years of slavery in the various parts of the Americas?

7. Who were Gabriel Prosser, Denmark Vesey, and Nat Turner? What is the significance of their acts?

8. What is that "something much bigger than history itself" which emerges as the major point in this article on the African background and the slave trade?

1. Find out as much as you can about Estevanico. Be on the lookout particularly for information as to his status in the eyes of the Spaniards and the Indians. (That is, was he considered "different" because of his race? If so, was the reaction to the difference generally negative, positive, or objective?)

2. Do some supplementary reading on the rise of the plantation economy in the West Indies and in the United States. Compare the two with respect to the treatment of the slaves (work load, cultural outlets, for example) and the mingling of the races (status of mulattos, for example).

3. Nat Turner, because of the tremendous implications of his deed, has not always been written about with complete objectivity. Read several works on Nat Turner. How many different portraits can you draw of him based on what you have read. Write out as many brief, concise, and objective descriptions of him, his character, and his actions as your readings warrant, and compare them. (Be sure to learn something of the author of each account.)

4. Do some reading on the abortive revolt led by Denmark Vesey. What parallels and contrasts can you draw between Nat Turner's conspiracy and that of Vesey?

5. The Catholic Church intervened quite often in the fifteenth and sixteenth centuries in fixing the position of Europeans toward the institution of slavery. If edited or indexed versions of papal encyclicals (official pronouncements of the popes) are available to you, read those sections which deal with the African slave trade. (If you wish to pursue the topic further, you might read also those which deal with the enslavement of Indians. In this case you may need to know something of papal politics and of the role of Bartolomé de las Casas, Spanish bishop of Chiapas.)

Suggested Readings

The Peculiar Institution. By Kenneth M. Stampp. Vintage Book, Random House, New York, 1964. See chapters one through four.

The Negro in the Making of America. By Benjamin Quarles. Collier, New York, 1964. A good overview of Black American History.

The Negro in the United States. A Brief History. By Rayford W. Logan. Van Nostrand, Princeton, N.J., 1947.

Capitalism and Slavery. By Eric Williams. Capricorn Books. New York, 1966. See especially chapters five through ten.

Before The Mayflower. By Lerone Bennett. Penguin, Baltimore, 1966. A very readable history of Black America.

PART II: The SCHOLARS' APPANAGE:

SUPPLEMENTAL LESSONS IN SLAVERY AND THE AFRICAN SLAVETRADE

PLANTATION ECONOMY: THE ISLAND CASE

Lloyd Best

I intend to present a caricature of how plantation economy first arose in the Caribbean and then fell. I'm not dealing in history, but in theater. My treatment will be a little elliptical, a little allegorical, if you like, and it is for you, as in all theater, to fill in the gaps.

Let us begin with a flight of fantasy. Imagine that we are transported back into the fifteenth century, somewhere on the North Atlantic seaboard. Around us there is a bustling metropolis, a civilization arising out of the Middle Ages. Skeptical scholars are everywhere asking frank questions and reviving classical knowledge. The church is being forced to relax its hold on the inquring mind; great strides are being made in geography and engineering, and in the establishment of a technological civilization.

The commercial classes are freeing themselves from feudal interference; impetus is being given to technology that will better equip them to search for profitable trade. At their disposal are better charts, better maps, bigger and sturdier ships, and better firearms.

After centuries of frustration, hope is now turning into expectation. Islam has been driven back. Moral, commercial, and technical considerations blend as men sweep outward beyond the sea. It is exploration, war, and trade to the east and west as explorers are scrambling for advantage.

A rare photograph taken in 1847 of a group of recently purchased Africans with their enslavers in Martinique. (*Roger Jean Segalat*)

Let us invite the Pope to be arbiter in a rivalry over east and west. Let us now follow the fortunes of the west. According to the sailors' yarns, there lies beyond the horizon to the west a multitude of islands, some much like the Azores. Of special appeal was the Antilles, lost isles of the Seven Cities. One of the sailors had a special mission—Columbus wanted to go to east by west. He would get to India, he said, or, if not, he would at least discover new lands. We now start with our first formal assumption, this bit of historical theater set, of course, in the framework of economics.

In the beginning, there was the hinterland. And in the center of the world there are the metropolises, centers of mercantile enterprise, of business organizations, technology, finance, and all the services required for production and trade.

Then there was the east and the west to be exploited, and mercantile enterprise could undertake the business of extracting supplies to be traded for profit in the metropolis. It is of little importance what the supplies were—minerals, forest produce, furs, or agriculture produce such as sugar, cotton, and tobacco. The main consideration was that they were to be extracted.

Our second assumption is that the aim of the enterprise in the hinterlands was to make a profit that was transferable to the metropolis.

Our third assumption concerns the length of the profit horizon. In a mercantile enterprise, undertaken between a metropolis and a remote, uncharted territory, this must necessarily be short. The surplus must not only be adequate and transferable, but it must materialize quickly.

What these three key assumptions add up to is that the initiators of the enterprise do not have as their main purpose taking up permanent residence in the hinterlands, or founding a society in which they and their fellow men could live.

Our fourth assumption concerns the way in which such a society and economy could be established. For the purpose of extracting the maximum surplus in a short time, the ideal form of organization is an institution, such as the plantation, which for all practical purposes is self-sufficient. It must have its own resident labor force, which implies slavery or some strict form of labor indenture. If it provides its own consumption supplies, its own equipment, and all the ancillary services from within the organization, the managers and the senior staff are able to minimize the cost of subsistence of the inmates (in this case the slaves) and to direct the energies of the enterprise to producing the surplus. This pure form is, of course, possible only in the case of a hinterland that is virtually uninhabited and/or in which indigenous military and cultural resistance is so weak that the population can readily be incorporated into total institutions such as the plantation.

This neatly corresponds to the Caribbean Case. The lands of the Antilles, which Columbus found, proved not to have seven glittering cities as imagined, but a sprinkling of poorly organized American Indians. For a plantation economy, labor had to be brought in from outside. And labor could here be contained and controlled, all the easier for two reasons: First, it had no cultural base in the new country; and second, the country was an island, which restricted the possibility of large-scale flight of the labor force.

Plantation economy had no market for labor and, indeed, no market for goods or for capital. Each plantation did business only with the metropolitan merchant house or company, its parent and sponsor. Only the merchant house received the trading opportunity. It provided the initial investment, the techniques of production, and the managerial and technical skills needed. It provided the plantation with the supplies and services needed to carry on production. As produce began to flow, the merchant house received the surplus merchandise, organized transportation for it, and provided for the final sale.

When all the important connections were between single plantations and their metropolitan sponsors, the economy had to be held

41

together by whatever legal and political system the planters could devise to bolster the social and moral order within each plantation. In this sense, only the plantation society had to have a government.

A fifth assumption relates to the character of government in this kind of society, that is, a society dominated by the plantation. The role of government is to maintain law and order. Its terms of reference are set by the plantation. Its resources in men and equipment are provided as needed. Being the supreme authority, in some sense it necessarily has also a military task; but its civil tasks are quite distinctive, specific, and narrowly circumscribed. The major civil task of government is the regulation of ownership and use of land. Not that there is any market for land as such; in the nature of plantation economy, there is no property right for the working population. If land were available to them, they could simply clear land and claim it for themselves. On the ground that it must prevent this, plantation economy has a planter government.

Before we examine the working of such an economy, it is necessary to spell out some other assumptions. The internal stability of the plantation, and therefore of its society, requires a convergence between the values of the slaves or indentured workers and what actual behavior is demanded of them.

Most members of the labor force adapt to the culture and style of plantation life. We may expect this all the more if, as in the Caribbean case, they are initially recruited from outside, for then they are cut off from their own culture without having the opportunity to integrate themselves into the indigenous culture, and the biological, social, and economic processes within the plantation economy and society are just flexible enough to admit some social mobility and to promise a lot more without posing any immediate threat to the established order.

It needs to be stressed, however, that this is merely a reasonable presumption. What actually happens depends on a number of factors, including the sharpness of the cultural and ideological conflict between the working population and the staff, the effectiveness of social controls, the type of military opportunities opened by the terrain, and so on. If the labor force is indentured, as in the case of, say, Virginia, the terms of the indenture may also be decisive in leading to the rapid breakdown of the initial form.

In any event, it is entirely likely that a spirit of resentment against the required routine and patterns of behavior will prevail and express itself in perverse behavior; even if the established order survives, normal behavior will at best be ambivalent. Conformist tendencies will of course be open and dissenting tendencies disguised. The typical slave will behave differently depending on the situation in which he finds himself. The untypical ones who wish

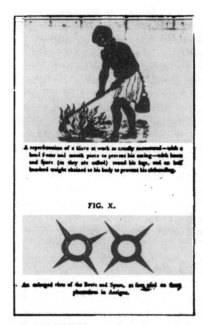

FIG. X.

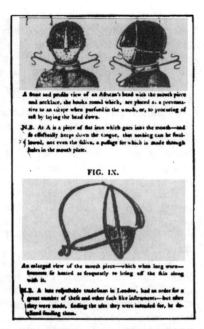

FIG. IX.

These instruments were created and used to further subjugate the Africans to their captive bondage and thus subdue any rebellious force within them.   (*Rare Book Division, New York Public Library*)

to dissent openly will be quickly suppressed or they might simply make a dash for it and run away. If they are successful, we then have the phenomenon of Maroons.

Within the plantation itself, the requirements for maintenance of social order discriminate against innovation. Established routines are too important to the preservation of order to be changed.

This yields our seventh and eighth assumptions. Consumer tastes among the laborers will tend to be fixed to match the initial pattern of supplies, and the initial techniques of production and the initial structure of skills will tend to remain rigid. Where the profit horizon is extremely short, where the process of production is simply a matter of putting unskilled laborers to work on land, maintaining them at the lowest possible rations and creaming off the surplus, we may articulate a ninth and tenth assumption that the plantation will employ only two factors of production: land and capital, capital in the form of slaves which they own.

To sum up the assumptions, we have an economy comprised of a series of plantations producing a single crop for export. It is tied to the metropolis by the link between the planting staff and the merchant houses.

43

Now let us look at the operation of this plantation economy; we're now in a position to do so, having set out the assumptions. The economy is of course almost exclusively a trading economy. All produce not consumed on the plantation is exported. All supplies not produced on the plantation are imported. The most important determinant of the viability of the business is the terms on which trade takes place. Of course, it is pointless to apply tests of viability only at the level of the plantation economy. We must also consider the entire metropolitan merchant enterprise, including all its affiliates. It would be pointless for the planters to produce only for home consumption; this would deny the plantation's very reason for being. There would be no surplus which could be transferred to the metropolises to discharge the mounting liabilities there.

First, what the planters can do when they're in trouble is to switch from one export to another. Second, they could produce more consumer supplies that could substitute for imports. Third, they could use their labor more efficiently to increase production of the traditional exports.

Finally, when worse comes to worst, the planter consumes capital. What does this mean? First, he may borrow to feed his slaves or, more likely, feed them rations that are below subsistence; or, he may cut costs by working the slaves harder for the same rations. So long as slaves are cheap and profits can be expected to recover, neither solution is completely unworkable. But by overworking or underfeeding his slaves, the planter runs the risk of increasing costs, delaying recovery, and impairing the maintenance of law and order.

The slave survived an insurmountable amount of barbarous treatment. The use of the treadwheel was one punitive measure.
(*The Mansell Collection*)

Borrowing to feed the slaves may be the superior course of action, even if it requires mortgaging future income. Fortunately, depressions during the golden age are more than cancelled by booms.

One result of good profits in the first phase of plantation economy is the emergence of a wealthy elite, composed of both merchants and planters; the elite develop a taste for splendor and good living. A second consequence of high profits is a switch of the entrepreneurial role from the merchant to the planter. With the expansion that marks this phase, merchants need high liquidity to service new business, and at times, the planters buy the assets of the plantation from themselves.

A third important consequence is a combination of the first two. Several factors cooperate to establish high living standards for the planters, among them the habits of their own class in better days. This means that consumption expenditures now take on the character of a fixed charge on plantation accounts.

But it is with the passing of the golden age that this and other inflexibilities begin to tell against the survival of the system.

Finally, in the hinterland economy, maturation sets in. This means, first of all, that soil exhaustion contributes to mounting costs. Shifting onto new terrain and the breaking of fresh land is difficult, especially on an island.

So, for output to rise, more slave labor must be applied to a given acreage and to well-used land. What is more, slaves are now harder to procure; expansion in the good days has induced rising prices, and costs now also begin to mount. The emergence of the industrial classes, and the wealth created for the metropolitan economy by the

Sugar cultivation was the prime industry in the West Indies; here the labo ers prepare the land for planting. Most work gangs contained both men and women performing equal workloads. (*Library of Congress*)

plantation, brings social turmoil into metropolitan society, and with that, war between metropolitan societies on a larger scale than before. Now the theme, of course, is war, more exploration, new trade.

Still further, export prices begin to tumble as the expansion of the system brings an oversupply to the market in the metropolis. Besides war between metropolises, plantations are changing hands and markets are being dislocated. The change in the mercantile enterprise, as market prices worsen and merchants increase margins on their own defense, is reflected externally in sharply deteriorating trade.

Internally, it is reflected in chronic unemployment. The planters fall back on the patterns of adjustment they had learned during the temporary depressions of the golden age. But by now the depression is a bottomless trough. They cannot easily sell, and they can hardly even borrow. Thus, they now consume capital in two ways, both by borrowing to continue their own style of life and by underfeeding and overworking the slaves. Economic depression is followed by social and political instability. To give the slaves land and a chance to enter the system on equal terms and to give them time to produce their own food is to disrupt the established order and to encourage dissent. Not to give this to them is to court revolt. What is more, some side effects of borrowing compound the instability. Persistent slum conditions bring foreclosures against plantation property. The planters are trapped. Their only recourse is through metropolitan help. Help first, in the form of market regulations; but this is too much in conflict with the interests of the industrial class who are in command of the system and are all too strong to be denied. Help secondly, with the maintenance of law and order; this seems admissible; but then, as it becomes a permanent charge on the metropolitan government account, with chronic slum conditions and permanent instability in plantation economy, the metropolis has no choice but to intervene and restore order.

That is the story. What is the moral? Briefly, the rigid plantation form of social and economic organization, which persistently discriminates against initiative by the population at the bottom and is totally dependent on metropolitan forces, necessarily faces the choice of either total breakdown or of metropolitan intervention to keep order.

I suggest without elaboration that this analytical caricature, necessarily restricted here to plantation economy—this caricature of the early history of the Caribbean—provides important clues to the economic predicament of the rural plantation economy that exists in the Caribbean today and its sister economies which may exist in other parts of the continent.

I have said nothing about the way in which the early plantation form has been transformed in the contemporary period, the way in which the sugar plantation has been supplanted by bauxite and petroleum corporations. I leave it to you to make the links and to discern what this means for the Caribbean economy. What does this heritage of plantation economy, which is so rigid that it's not able to permit flexible development, imply for the whole Afro-American community?

Exercises

Questions for Discussion

1. Describe the intellectual and cultural climate existing in Europe in the late fifteenth and early sixteenth centuries which precipitated the outward movement for exploration, trade, and conquest.

2. Explain the significance of the terms "metropolis" and "hinterland." What is their relationship to each other?

3. Define the term "plantation." What conditions are prerequisite to the establishment of a plantation?

4. What tools, skills, and services does the metropolis supply to the plantation? To what end?

5. What is the principle characteristic of "planter government"?

6. "The internal stability of the plantation . . . requires a convergence between the values of the slaves or indentured workers and the actual behavior demanded of them in the process of production." Does such a convergence of values depend to any degree on external factors, such as topography, proximity of the slave population to its cultural roots, and so forth?

7. Professor Best gives ten assumptions in his presentation of island plantation economy. Can you list at least five of them?

8. Name six alternatives open to the planter when demand in the metropolis for his goods markedly decreases and he is faced with depression.

9. In the mature phase of the plantation economy, after the golden age has passed, what factors contribute principally to the deterioration of the system? Is there a cause and effect progression? What role does plantation inflexibility play in the ultimate demise of the system?

10. Can the cycle repeat itself (can the system be reborn) at a later age? Can you draw a systematic parallel between a sugar planta-

tion economy and the organization and routine of the modern petroleum corporation and its installations?

Activities

1. The major civil task of the planter government has been defined as the regulation of the ownership and use of land. Read briefly through some of the land tenure bills considered in either house of the Virginia legislature during the time that slavery was becoming a fixed and permanent part of the law (in the 1680s and 1690s). Can you discern the characteristic point of view of "planter government" through these bills?

2. Corporations quite often prepare public relations material on their operations. Find out what bauxite and petroleum firms based in the United States have operations in the West Indies, and find out whether they provide public relations literature regarding their operations. If so, what kind of information is stressed in this literature? (In what kinds of journals would you be likely to find advertisements by such firms?)

3. Describe a typical day, using your imagination to supply fictional characters and episodes, in the life of an eighteenth century plantation either in the West Indies, or in Virginia or the Carolinas. Describe the same events first from the point of view of the owner, and then from the point of view of the field hand.

Suggested Readings

History of the People of Trinidad and Tobago. By Eric Williams. PNM Publishing Co., Ltd.,Port-of-Spain, Trinidad, W.I., 1962. Also contains very good information on the West Indies in general.

British Historians and the West Indies. By Eric Williams. PNM Publishing Co., Ltd., Port-of-Spain, Trinidad, W.I., 1964. A concise book about the British interpreters of West Indian history.

Documents of West Indian History 1492–1655. By Eric Williams. PNM Publishing Co., Ltd., Port-of-Spain, Trinidad, W.I., 1963. Documents relating to the history of the West Indies. The documents on the voyages are quite revealing.

Democracy and Empire in the Caribbean. By Paul Blanshard. New York, 1947. A survey history of the West Indies.

The European Nations in the West Indies 1493–1688. By A. P. Newton. Barnes & Noble, New York, 1967. A good general history of the development of European colonialism in the West Indies.

SLAVERY IN THE SOUTHERN
COLONIES FROM 1619 TO 1776

Edgar A. Toppin

One of the interesting dates in American history is 1619. In that year, the Virginia colony received its first batch of women, received a legislature beginning self-government in the American colonies, and, it is generally believed, received the first batch of Africans. That date, 1619, for the first coming of Africans to the English colonies is interesting because it antedates the coming of the *Mayflower* in 1620. The fact that Black people came to Jamestown colony is established in a letter written by John Rolfe, who introduced tobacco and married Pocahontas, to Sir Edwin Sandys, the treasurer of the London company that controlled the colony of Jamestown.

In this letter he said that in August of 1619 a Dutch man-of-war arrived at Point Comfort with about twenty Negroes, which the governor bought "for victuals . . . at the best and easiest rates they could."

The letter established that Black men came to Jamestown in 1619. But the question is, what was the status of these Africans at that time? Many people have mistakenly assumed that they were slaves from the start, but it appears that they were instead regarded as indentured servants.

The English, lacking the continuous experience with slavery that the Portuguese and Spaniards of the Iberian peninsula had had, did not have a ready-made set of slave laws to carry over into the New World. Slavery had ended in England around 1000 A.D., so laws in regard to slavery no longer existed; therefore, the colonists had to find their way by a process of trial and error. Thus, slavery developed haltingly and gradually, and only after they had tried other alternatives. Faced with the problem of labor, they first attempted the use of Indian and White indentured servants. They soon found that the Indians did not make satisfactory slaves because the Indian men were not accustomed to the arduous labor involved in farming; the Indian men had left that work to the women, while they concentrated on hunting and warfare.

They continued to use White indentured servants for a considerable period of time; as late as 1671, there were some 6000 White indentured servants in Virginia, and only 2000 Africans. So that slavery developed only gradually, and as a substitute, as they learned that the Black slaves, who had been accustomed to farming in Africa, made much more useful workers around farms and plantations.

By 1624, the census figures showed 25 Africans in the colony. Some of these, at least, were regarded as indentured servants, and when they had served their terms, they became free individuals and landowners and themselves holders of indentured servants.

Some people assumed that slavery in Virginia did not develop until the first laws were passed in regard to slavery. But the truth of the matter is that there were customs and court rulings that indicated that some Africans, at least, had begun to be held as slaves as early as the 1640s. Some of them were held to life tenure; and if a man owned you for life, rather than for the limited term of an indentured servant, then you obviously came under the status of slave.

Among these first Africans in the New World, two were involved in the first case that established a basis for slavery in Virginia. One of these was Anthony Johnson, who had arrived on one of the earliest ships (probably the one that came in in 1622), and went on to become a free person after serving out his period of indenture. Then he began to own indentured servants himself, settling in a colony with other former Black indentured servants in Virginia. Another man named Casor, who was owned by Anthony Johnson as an indentured servant, complained to some White men in the colony that Anthony Johnson continued to hold him as a servant after he had finished his indenture and therefore should be set free, as Anthony Johnson himself had been set free. Casor asked these Whites to help him bring pressure against Anthony Johnson, and Anthony Johnson then allowed Casor to leave his premises. But the two White men took Casor and held him as their servant, whereupon

Anthony Johnson, saying, "Well, if he's going to be an indentured servant, he might as well be mine," went into court. The judge decided that Casor should be returned to Johnson and should be his servant for life. That was the first recorded civil case in the history of Virginia establishing a person as a slave for life. That was in the mid-1650s.

Earlier, there was a criminal court case in which two White indentured servants and a Negro ran away together, and they were captured and brought before the judge. The ruling was that the two White indentured servants were to serve longer terms as punishment for running away. But, the court ruling went on, since the Black man could not be made to serve any additional years, therefore he was to be punished by a whipping—indicating that this man was already a servant for life, so they couldn't add any more years to his term.

But as yet, there were no laws explicitly establishing slavery in Virginia.

Now let's look at some of the provisions of the statutes that did begin the establishment of slavery in Virginia. The first of these statutes, passed in 1661, provided that in case any White indentured servant ran away with any Negroes, who were incapable of making satisfaction by addition of time, that the English servant shall serve time for the absent Negroes. That law is regarded as the first one to indicate that Black slavery existed in Virginia. In 1662 another law was passed that carried the process a step beyond by stating that the status of all children born in Virginia would be determined according to the condition of the mother. This was significant because in England, under common law, a child took the status of the father. Thus White men were free to have relations with their Black indentured servants, or slaves, and the child became a slave; White men could thus add to their stock of slaves by procreating with their slave women.

In 1667 a statute was passed to resolve the problem of whether or not conversion to Christianity would free a person from being a slave; the statute stated that the conferring of baptism does not alter the condition of the person as to his bondage or freedom. Now a master freed from this doubt, could continue the propagation of the faith and could still keep a person as a slave even if he converted him to Christianity.

In 1670 another law provided that all servants not being Christians imported into Virginia by ship were to be held as slaves for life. The only people coming into Virginia by ship who weren't Christians were Blacks from Africa. The law also went on to say that such servants as came by land were to serve, if boys and girls, until 30 years of age; if men or women, twelve years, and no longer.

But there was one more step in the process of degrading the

51

NEGROES
FOR
SALE

A CARGO OF *very stout Men and Women, in good order and fit for immediate service, just imported from the Windward Coast of Africa, in the Ship* TWO BROTHERS.

Conditions are one half Cash or Produce, the other half payable the first of January next, giving Bond and Security if required.

May 19, 1784   *John C. Mitchell*

A notice announcing the arrival of Africans as slaves.
(*Negro History Associates*)

Black man. In 1705, a law was passed by the General Assembly of Virginia stating that all Negro, mulatto, and Indian slaves shall be held, taken, and adjudged to be real estate, in the same category as livestock and household furniture, wagons, and goods.

These laws indicate that Virginia was moving more and more toward slavery. One of the factors causing this was the decline in the available supply of indentured servants. Europe had provided White indentured servants for the colonies, not only by the voluntary process of signing up for labor to make up the cost of passage, but also by kidnapping individuals from the streets. Parents might send a child to the store and never see him again—because the child had been kidnapped and sent to the colonies.

Judges often gave criminals a choice of going to jail or going to America. (Some preferred jail.) But in the 1670s, England began passing laws that made it more difficult to kidnap people to sell into indentured servitude. In addition, the freedom dues, the sum of money paid an indentured servant at the end of his service, were becoming higher and higher because the supply of indentured servants was dwindling.

As it became more expensive to obtain indentured servants, the colony turned more and more to Africans. In the eighteenth century, the number of Africans in Virginia increased considerably; by 1712, there were 12,000 Blacks to 18,000 Whites in the colony, and most of the 12,000 Blacks were slaves.

Virginia eventually had the largest Black population of all the colonies. In 1756 there were 170,000 Whites and 120,000 Blacks; which means that the Blacks comprised 41 percent of the population. In fact, Virginia, as a colony and as a state, remained tops in Black population for decades. The 1860 census showed that there were more Blacks living in Virginia than in any other colony or state within what became the United States of America. It wasn't until the 1870 census that Georgia passed Virginia, becoming the state with the most Blacks.

In Maryland, slavery existed almost from the start. Maryland was founded in 1634 as a refuge for Catholics, and the proprietors and residents evidently permitted slavery from the beginning. Maryland lagged in passage of laws about slavery, but from all of the available records, the Blacks who were living there were regarded as slaves from the time they first arrived in the 1630s.

The next colony we will consider is Carolina; I say "Carolina" because South Carolina and North Carolina were one colony, a colony granted to eight proprietors by a charter from the English king in 1663. However, some people from Virginia had moved into what is now North Carolina as early as 1654. The first residents sent over under the terms of the charter went, in 1670, to Charlestown, in what became South Carolina.

John Locke, the great English philosopher, was selected by the

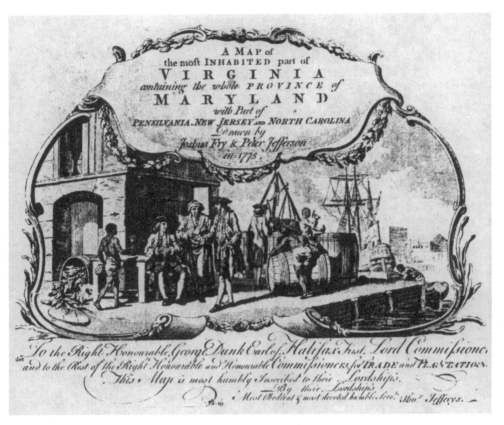

A MAP of
the most INHABITED part of
VIRGINIA
containing the whole PROVINCE of
MARYLAND
with Part of
PENSILVANIA, NEW JERSEY and NORTH CAROLINA
Drawn by
Joshua Fry & Peter Jefferson
in 1775

To the Right Honourable, George Dunk Earl of Halifax First Lord Commissione[r]
and to the Rest of the Right Honourable and Honourable Commissioners for TRADE and PLANTATION.
This Map is most humbly Inscribed to their Lordships.
By their Lordships
Most Obedient & most devoted humble Serv.t Thos Jefferys.

America's early dealings with slavery sent most of the newly arrived Africans to the South to work the vast stretches of fertile land. (*New York Historical Society*)

proprietors to prepare a constitution for the Carolinas, and in this constitution he provided for slavery, under the terms of which Africans would be held under the absolute control of their masters.

South Carolina developed a large population of slaves, mostly men from Africa, for several reasons. One, they developed a rice culture and needed slaves to work on the plantations. Another reason was that the proprietors were themselves directors of the Royal African Company, which was the main English slave-trading company; in fact, it had a monopoly for a considerable time. So these proprietors wore two hats: As proprietors of a colony, they were interested in the colony's welfare; but as directors of the Royal African Company, they were interested in selling slaves. So the area that became South Carolina developed a very large slave population. In fact, by 1763, there were only 30,000 Whites compared with 70,000 Blacks—70 percent of the population. This was the only colony that had more Blacks than Whites.

This being the case, fears developed in South Carolina about the large number of Blacks; and strict codes were passed, codes designed to keep slaves from possessing firearms, from striking back at their masters, from rebelling. But even these codes did not prevent a rebellion from taking place in South Carolina—the most startling rebellion in the entire colonial period.

It took place in 1739 at Stono Plantation, near Charleston, South Carolina, and it's known as Cato's Conspiracy. A group of slaves broke into a storeroom, where they seized arms and ammunition, and began marching on their way to freedom in Florida, attacking and plundering houses as they went. But the countryside was aroused, and, finally, they were caught and defeated. In that uprising, some 30 Whites and 44 Blacks were killed.

What is now North Carolina did not develop very many slaves because it had smaller farms, tobacco farms rather than the large rice plantations. The people there were not so prosperous or wealthy or aristocratic; so North Carolina had one of the smallest slave populations among the Southern colonies. In fact, by 1760, North Carolina had only 77,000 Whites and only 16,000 Blacks—17 percent of the population.

The colony of Georgia was founded in 1733 as a refuge for debtors. James Oglethorpe and the other proprietors were interested in

Tobacco proved to be a profitable export; thus, the captive laborers worked to cultivate and expand this crop. *(Culver Pictures, Inc.)*

helping that group of unfortunates. But it was also designed as a buffer colony to protect South Carolina from attacks from the Indians and Spaniards in Florida.

The proprietors, working to keep the people of Georgia on an even keel, decided to prohibit individual land ownership, to prohibit the sale of alcoholic beverages, and to prohibit the holding of slaves. Now all three of these prohibitions went strongly against the grain of the American character. Almost from the beginning, the Georgia colonists began to protest against not being allowed to own land privately—they were supposed to own it collectively and work for the company. They protested against not being able to have liquor, and they strongly protested against not being able to have slaves.

The proprietors had a Utopian notion that these people could work on things such as manufacturing of silk and other exotic goods, but the whole experiment broke down. The people of Georgia began to get around the prohibition against slavery by renting slaves from slave-owners of South Carolina on 100-year leases.

In 1742 the prohibition against private land holding was dropped. In 1749 the prohibition against having slaves was dropped. In 1750 the prohibition against liquor was dropped. Then the people of Georgia were able to enjoy those three things as the people in other colonies did.

This, then, is the beginning of slavery in the Southern colonies.

Exercises

Questions for Discussion

1. By what evidence has it been established that Black men landed in the United States in 1619?

2. What arguments have been advanced in support of the view that those Africans were regarded as indentured servants rather than as slaves?

3. At about what date are there indications that practices of slavery, or practices tantamount to slavery, are being instituted? What form do these practices take?

4. Why is the name Anthony Johnson important in the history of slavery in the United States?

5. Dr. Toppin states that no provisions for slavery existed in Virginia at the time of the initial arrival of Blacks and that the colony

found its way slowly and gropingly toward a system of slavery. Describe some of the laws passed in Virginia in the second half of the seventeenth century that demonstrate this. Does the wording of the laws seem to indicate any ambivalence on the part of the legislators as to the institution of slavery on an explicit, legal basis? Compare this situation with that of Maryland and of the Carolinas.

6. Which Southern state had the largest Black population during the period before the Civil War? In which Southern state did Blacks comprise the largest percentage of the total population?

7. Give two reasons why the southern part of Carolina developed a large population of slaves? Why was the situation different in the northern part of Carolina?

8. What three prohibitions went into the constitution of the colony of Georgia? How did the colonists react to these prohibitions? Did they find means to circumvent any of them?

9. What crops originally formed the basis of the economy of the Southern colonies? What kind of labor is necessary (that is, manpower volume, skill, and so forth) to tend and harvest such crops?

Activities

1. John Locke, the philosopher who drew up the constitution for the Carolinas, is known as the proponent of empiricism, of the observation of the natural world. His major work is *An Essay Concerning Human Understanding.* Consult an encyclopedia for a summary of his system. Pay particular attention to his views on moral philosophy. Are they compatible with slavery?

2. Do some research on tobacco and rice production in the United States at present. Compare your results with the descriptions you find in history books of the method of growing these crops in colonial America.

3. Consult relief maps and weather maps of the Southern part of the United States (the area included in the states of Delaware, Virginia, North and South Carolina, Georgia, Alabama, Mississippi, and Louisiana). Determine the typical topography and climate for these regions. Consult agricultural maps and census reports. Determine what crops are currently grown in these areas. What other large industry or industries operate in these areas?

Suggested Readings

Slavery in the Americas: A Comparative Study of Cuba and Virginia. By Herbert S. Klein. The University of Chicago Press, Chicago, 1967.

A History of Negro Slavery in New York. By Edgar J. McManus. The first general history of slavery in New York State and how it developed.

Slave and Citizen: The Negro in the Americas. By Frank Tannenbaum. Vintage Book, Random House, New York, 1946.

The Peculiar Institution: Slavery in the Ante-Bellum South. By Kenneth M. Stampp. Vintage Book, Random House, New York, 1956. A general history of slavery in America that attempts to consider the feelings of the slaves.

The Political Economy of Slavery. By Eugene D. Genovese. Pantheon, New York, 1965. Studies in the economy and society of the slave era in the South.

SLAVERY IN THE NORTHERN COLONIES FROM 1624 TO 1776

Edgar A. Toppin

Sometimes people assume, quite erroneously, that slavery existed only in the South. There was a good deal of slavery in the North as well. Let us take a look at the New England and Middle Atlantic colonies and see how slavery developed in those areas and how the economics of the region, the geography and the climate, affected the development of slavery there.

We're going to begin with four colonies in New England: Massachusetts, New Hampshire, Connecticut, and Rhode Island.

What is now Maine was part of Massachusetts until 1820. In this colonial period, Vermont was not a separate colony; it became a separate state in 1777. At this time, what is now Vermont was claimed by both New Hampshire and New York. And that's why we're dealing with only four colonies—Massachusetts, which included Maine; New Hampshire, which included Vermont; Connecticut; and Rhode Island.

Slavery in the New England colonies is associated primarily with Massachusetts. Although Rhode Island had the largest percentage of Blacks for most of the colonial period, Massachusetts had more slaves, although not very many more, than the other colonies.

Massachusetts was founded in 1620, when the Pilgrims, or Separatists, came to Plymouth on the *Mayflower*. The much larger body, the Puritans, came to the Massachusetts Bay region in 1630. From Massachusetts, the first of the New England colonies, the other colonies developed.

We do not know just when the first Blacks were brought to Massachusetts colony and African slavery began there. Most historians accept the date 1638 because then there definitely were some African slaves. But there's a possibility that African slaves may have been in Massachusetts as early as 1624 or 1625; a colonist living there then was known as a slave trader and owner, although the records are not clear on this point.

For the people of Massachusetts to hold slaves posed a problem, since they were Puritans; Puritan divines, with their strong sense of religion, had to raise the question of whether or not they could properly possess slaves. So they resolved that problem by deciding that Africans were a degraded, accursed, despised race which they could assist—they could civilize them by holding them as slaves and introducing them to the benefits of the Western culture.

That sort of rationalization was convenient. But the game was given away by other statements of people of the Massachusetts colony, such as Governor John Winthrop, arguing that the Massachusetts Bay colony would never prosper as well as other colonies without slaves to do the labor to make money for the colonists living there. Economic gain motivated the existence of slavery in this region. In terms of climate, however, the rather severe winters, the rather rocky soil, except in a few places such as the Connecticut River Valley, forced the colonists in Massachusetts to have small farms. In fact, as they moved out to establish new communities, they moved whole townships at a time. The small farms, clustered around the small towns, did not have the need for slave labor the way it was needed on the large plantations in the South.

Instead, the slaves in Massachusetts were used more in urban settings, as dockworkers or as household servants. Some were used in farming but not many. So, in the New England region, slavery did not take on—not because the people were more humane or noble or had a greater idealistic sense in regard to slavery, but simply because there was not the same economic necessity for it.

Massachusetts, in 1755, had 195,000 Whites and only 4800 Blacks—only 2 percent of the population. In the South, the colony with the smallest proportion of slaves, North Carolina, had 17 percent.

Connecticut became a colony when people moved out from Massachusetts Bay and settled along the Connecticut River Valley where the soil was very fertile. Although they had some encounters with the Dutch there, they established various towns, beginning in 1635, such as Windsor, Hartford, Wethersfield, and New Haven. The people of Connecticut found slaves to be useful in their farming operations, and eventually they had a larger proportion of slaves than in Massachusetts (although not nearly so many, because Connecticut was a smaller colony). In 1756, Connecticut had 128,000 Whites and 3600 Blacks—3 percent of the population.

The colony in the New England region that really had a large percentage of Africans was little Rhode Island. Now, Rhode Island was founded by people who were unable to accept the religious control of the Puritans of Massachusetts, the degree to which this control carried over into governmental matters, and the relations with the Indians. One of these people, Roger Williams, was expelled from the colony and moved to Rhode Island in 1636. Another was Anne Hutchinson, who was expelled from the colony because she insisted on personal interpretation of the Bible, believing that she could thus have a more direct relationship with God than through the Puritan divines.

So various people left Massachusetts Bay as dissenters and settled at places such as Newport and Providence and the Narragansett Bay region. Rhode Island was settled by people, such as Roger Williams, who had a strong sense of democracy and fair play. Roger Williams was one of the most noble of early Americans in terms of his humanitarian attitude toward Indians; he felt they should be dealt with fairly and be regarded as brothers. And yet, this man, the prime founder of Rhode Island, did permit slavery within the colony; and Rhode Island soon came to have a higher percentage of slaves than any of the other New England colonies.

This was primarily because Rhode Island was heavily engaged in the slave trade. Slave ships from Rhode Island, particularly from ports such as Newport, went over to the African coast, procured slaves, carried them to the West Indies for sale, and brought back from the West Indies not only the cash proceeds from the sale of slaves, but also sugar and molasses which were used to make rum, which was then carried, by this triangular route, back to Africa, because rum was one of the articles that was bartered to the African chiefs in exchange for slaves.

But the slave ships often came back from the West Indies with unsold slaves. These left over slaves gradually formed a large slave population. By 1755, Rhode Island had 4500 slaves in the colony at a time when there were only 36,000 White people—12 percent of the population of Rhode Island was Black, a Black population far larger than that of any other New England colony.

New Hampshire had a relatively small Black population; the lack of good ports for carrying on a slave trade—they were devoted more to a fishing economy—and the severity of the climate and the poor soil meant that New Hampshire had very little need for Africans. Again, very few were there not because of humanitarian instinct, but because they were not important to the economic system. So, in 1767, New

Hampshire had 52,000 Whites and only 633 Blacks—only 1 percent of the population.

In the New England region, slavery was in its mildest form; and slaves were treated better than in any other region. There was more opportunity for slaves to find kind masters, who might even provide some schooling for them. There was more opportunity for free Blacks living in this region to make some progress in life. But even so, there were still plots and revolts in New England, just as in other regions of the country.

In Connecticut there was a slave plot in the mid-1650s in Hartford. In Massachusetts there were slave plots at Newbury in the 1690s and at Charlestown in the 1740s.

Now let's consider slavery in the Middle Atlantic colonies of New York, Pennsylvania, and New Jersey. First, however, we should clear up the peculiar status of Delaware. Geographically, Delaware should be one of the Middle Atlantic colonies. In terms of politics, it belonged there because Delaware was controlled by Pennsylvania until early in the eighteenth century. Yet, Delaware was Southern in terms of its climate and its outlook—it had a tobacco economy. Delaware in 1790 had 46,000 Whites and 12,800 Blacks —22 percent of the population.

Now, let's look at New York. Some interesting things happened there. New York was settled first by the Dutch in 1624; the Dutch West India Company established a settlement on Manhattan Island subsequently known as New Amsterdam. The whole colony was called New Netherland. During the period of Dutch control, there was an interesting experiment in terms of usage of slaves. The Dutch developed a system known as half-freedom, by which a slave would be released by his master to earn a living and, in return, pay a certain price to his master each year on a contract basis. But, if he did not live up to his part of the agreement, he would be returned to his full status as a slave.

The Dutch West India Company, which controlled this benevolent colony, first began this system because they had too many slaves on the company's books—which was a fixed cost the company wanted to eliminate. They found that it would be cheaper to turn the slaves loose—while still keeping them tied to slavery by this half-freedom concept—and have the slaves pay the company for the privilege of earning the cost of their own housing, clothing, and feeding. But the key to this workable plan was that they got a great deal more productivity out of the slave that way. A man who has a chance to earn something for himself, even if it's very little, will work a great deal harder than a man who simply works for his master. The big problem under slavery was that there was no real incentive for the slave. This half-freedom system worked beautifully. Very seldom was a slave taken back from the half-freedom status and returned to slavery, because the slave enjoyed being out on his own, and he would work hard to make enough money to fulfill his part of the bargain.

Unfortunately, this system was not continued when the English seized New York from the Dutch in 1664. An expedition, sent out by King Charles II, was headed by the brother of the king, the Duke of York, who later became King James II. New Netherlands became New York.

Under the English slavery developed on a much larger scale than it had under the Dutch. The Dutch had treated the slaves almost as social equals. They *were* slaves; but there wasn't a constant reminder to the slave that he was degraded and humiliated. Now that was changed. The English promoted strict slavery. They developed it primarily because the Duke of York and the men who were associated with him in running the colony were also directors of the Royal African Company; therefore, just as was the case with the directors of the Royal African Company who were proprietors of South Carolina, it was to their benefit to push slavery. New York soon became the Northern colony with the largest number of slaves.

With the Royal African Company increasing the slave population, the same sort of fears that developed in South Carolina also developed in New York, and sometimes the slaves did things to justify those fears. For example, in 1712 there was a slave uprising. Some slaves assembled, with arms and ammunition, in the woods near New York City, where they set fire to a building. When Whites came to investigate the fire, the fight began. Eventually the slaves were subdued, and they were tried and hanged. Many innocent slaves were also hanged because of the panic that developed. This was significant, because several decades later, in 1741, what at first seemed to be an innocent matter blossomed into a sort of witch trial.

In the course of investigating a robbery, the New York authorities came across an indentured servant, a White woman named Mary Burton, who for some reason began to make claims about the tavern owner who was her master. She told the authorities that this man had been consorting with Blacks and plotting with Blacks. As the authorities became increasingly interested in her story, Mary, enjoying the attention, began making up wilder and wilder tales. They believed every bit of her story. As she accused more and more people, Blacks and Whites were jailed. The tavern owner and his wife were hanged. And many of the people who were brought in began telling on other people to save themselves. As these stories began to blossom and spread, panic ensued. Eventually, she began accusing prominent people who couldn't possibly have been involved in any plot of Whites and slaves to get together and overthrow New York. But the authorities couldn't tell the world that she had been lying, so, to save face, they passed an official resolution thanking her for helping save them from a plot which they now knew was

Constant unfounded rumors of slave rebellions in New York re-
sulted in this kind of mob action during 1741 and 1742.
(*Brown Brothers*)

A
JOURNAL
OF THE
PROCEEDINGS
IN
The Detection of the Conspiracy
FORMED BY
Some *White* People, in Conjunction with *Negro* and other *Slaves*,
FOR
Burning the City of *NEW-YORK* in AMERICA,
And Murdering the Inhabitants.

Which Conspiracy was partly put in Execution, by Burning His Majesty's House in Fort GEORGE, within the said City, on Wednesday the Eighteenth of *March*, 1741. and setting Fire to several Dwelling and other Houses there, within a few Days succeeding. And by another Attempt made in Prosecution of the same infernal Scheme, by putting Fire between two other Dwelling-Houses within the said City, on the Fifteenth Day of *February*, 1742; which was accidentally and timely discovered and extinguished.

CONTAINING,

I. A NARRATIVE of the Trials, Condemnations, Executions, and Behaviour of the several Criminals, at the Gallows and Stake, with their *Speeches* and *Confessions*; with Notes, Observations and Reflections occasionally interspersed throughout the Whole.

II. AN APPENDIX, wherein is set forth some additional Evidence concerning the said Conspiracy and Conspirators, which has come to Light since their Trials and Executions.

III. LISTS of the several Persons (Whites and Blacks) committed on Account of the Conspiracy; and of the several Criminals executed; and of those transported, with the Places whereto.

By the Recorder of the City of NEW-YORK.

Quid faciēnt Dŏmini, audent cum talia Fures? Virg. Ecl.

NEW-YORK:
Printed by *James Parker*, at the New Printing-Office, 1744.

nonexistent. And when she claimed the reward for her help, they had no choice but to pay her off.

In any case, New York, in 1756, had 83,000 Whites and 13,500 slaves—16 percent of the population. This was the largest number of slaves in any colony above the South.

New Jersey also had a large Black population. In 1745 there were 57,000 Whites and 4,700 Blacks—only 8 percent; but in the 1750s, New Jersey imported many more slaves and therefore had a much larger slave population.

Finally there was Pennsylvania, the colony of the gentle Quaker, William Penn. Despite his strong religious principles and his humanitarianism, Penn favored slavery. He felt that slaves were better than indentured servants since they were held for life, and he was pleased to have slavery introduced into his colony. This even though he was one of the most humane men in all of the colonies in terms of his treatment of other people and his ideas of religious freedom. But Pennsylvania became the colony where the first protest against slavery developed. By 1790, the time of the first census, Pennsylvania had 424,000 Whites and only 10,000 Blacks—2 percent of its population. So among the large Northern colonies, Pennsylvania had the smallest percentage of slaves in the population.

Exercises

Questions for Discussion

1. What rationalization did the Puritan ministers use to reconcile slavery with the Christian idea of humanity? Do you find anywhere in the Southern colonies a similar preoccupation with reconciling Christian charity and human bondage? Where? How did it manifest itself?

2. What kind of agricultural patterns were established in the North? Why? Did this affect the kind and volume of slavery there? How? (In what ways were slaves used?)

3. What was the percentage of Blacks in the total population in the middle of the eighteenth century in Massachusetts? In the northern part of Carolina? In Connecticut?

4. Why did Rhode Island have a greater proportion of slaves in relation to its total population than any other New England Colony? What was the percentage of Blacks in its population by 1755?

5. Why were there very few slaves in New Hampshire? What was their percentage in the total population?

6. What factors made Delaware a Northern state? What factors made it a Southern state?

7. Describe the system of "half freedom." Where and when was the system operative? How did it originate?

8. Why did the half-freedom system work more successfully than the full slave status?

9. What is the historical significance of Mary Burton?

10. William Penn favored slavery over indentured servitude, yet Pennsylvania had one of the smallest slave populations of the Northern colonies. Explain.

Activities

1. The period of Western history known as the Enlightenment occurred in the eighteenth century. Some men pondered such questions as knowledge, human liberty, and worth. Some of the men you have dealt with—Benjamin Franklin, John Locke—as well as others who are familiar to you (Thomas Jefferson, for instance) are generally regarded as belonging to this group of contemplative, ethical thinkers. Do some research on the period of the Enlightenment and on the specific position of the men named above. Curiously enough, all of these men favored African slavery. Can you think of reasons for the discrepancy?

2. Consult relief maps, weather maps, and so forth of the New England and Middle Atlantic states. Determine the topography and climate. Are there typical crops produced in these regions? What role does fishing play in regional economies? Shipping? Compare the industrial, agricultural, and commercial operations of this region with those of the South. What seem to be the major climactic and topographical differences between the two areas?

3. Compile a bibliography of abolitionist literature. Note especially the dates of publication and the places of publication. How many abolitionist tracts on your list were originally published in Pennsylvania?

4. Locate sermons by eighteenth century American Protestant ministers on the subject of slavery. Notice the way the sermons handle the subject. Are they pro? Con? Undecided? Are they pragmatic? Moralistic? Rationalistic? Consult books concerned with church history and the history of specific denominations.

Suggested Readings

From Slavery to Freedom: A History of Negro Americans. By John Hope Franklin. Vintage Book, Random House, New York, 1969. See chapters seven, eight, and nine.

A History of Negro Slavery in New York. By Edgar J. McManus. Syracuse University Press, Syracuse, N.Y., 1966.

American Negro Slavery: A Modern Reader. By Allen Weinstein and Frank Otto Gatell. Oxford University Press, New York, 1969. Twenty-two essays emphasizing the social issues involved in the slavery system.

Slavery: A Problem in American Institutional and Intellectual Life. By Stanley M. Elkins. Grossett & Dunlap, New York, 1963. A much consulted and somewhat controversial book on slavery and its impact on the Black personality.

The Shameful Trade. By F. George May. A. S. Barnes, Cranbury, N.J., 1967. A book about some of the most unpleasant aspects of the slave trade.

WHY THE UNITED STATES
DID NOT ABOLISH SLAVERY

Staughton Lynd

Why didn't the United States abolish slavery? The United States *did* abolish slavery in 1863 and in 1865. But why didn't the United States abolish slavery in 1776 at the time of the Declaration of Independence?

Or in 1787 when the Constitutional Convention met in Philadelphia to draft the United States Constitution?

Why didn't the United States abolish slavery at the time of the American Revolution, when there were about 500,000 slaves, rather than the four million that there were at the time of the Civil War?

Why didn't the United States abolish slavery at that moment when its founding manifesto proclaimed that all men are created equal?

When Abraham Lincoln said, in his Second Inaugural Address, that the Civil War would continue until every drop of blood that had been drawn by the lash was paid for with a drop of blood drawn by the sword, he spoke more wisely than he knew. For there had been half a million slaves in 1776, and more than half a million men had to die in the Civil War before slavery could end. Was this necessary? Why did the new country have to wait three-quarters of a century to destroy slavery?

This is not simply an academic question. Every bit of sensitivity and intuition that man possesses is required to answer a question like this. And, as with so many problems in the history of the Afro-American, there is a characteristic divergence of opinion between White and Black scholarship.

Let me contrast the work of two excellent scholars, one White and one Black. Professor Winthrop Jordan, a White historian, has recently published a magnificent scholarly work entitled *White Over Black*, a study of racial attitudes in the United States from the founding of the Colonies to the War of 1812. But let me quote from Professor Jordan's study, in referring to the Constitutional Convention of 1787: "Manifestly, the Convention could not consider even the eventual termination of domestic slavery." Why "manifestly"? He continues: "No one, of course, pondered the possibility of direct revolutionary action." Why "of course"? He says of the contrast between the natural-rights philosophy of the Declaration of Independence and the pragmatic philosophy of the Constitution: "During the postwar years, that is, the years following the end of the American Revolution . . . the Americans found that the philosophy of natural rights could not be made to serve as the cornerstone of effective government." Could not, or would not? And which Americans found that the natural-rights philosophy could not be made the basis of their government?

In contrast to this attitude, which seems to accept as inevitable the failure of the American Revolution to do something about slavery, let me quote from the great Black scholar W. E. B. Du Bois in his doctoral dissertation on the suppression of the African slave trade. In contrast to Professor Jordan's apparent acceptance of the Revolution's inability to take decisive action on this question, we find in the study by Du Bois such phrases as "energetic efforts were wanting," "there was a certain moral apathy," and "a fatal spirit of temporizing." And here is how Du Bois summed up his thoughts on the topic:

> We must face the fact that this problem arose principally from the cupidity and carelessness of our ancestors. It was the plain duty of the Colonies to crush the trade and the system in its infancy. They preferred to enrich themselves on its profits.
>
> It was the plain duty of a revolution based upon liberty to take steps toward the abolition of slavery. It preferred promises to straightforward action. It was the plain duty of the Constitutional Convention in founding a new nation to compromise with a threatening social evil only in case its settlement would thereby be postponed to a more favorable time. This was not the case in the slavery and the slave trade compromises.
>
> There never was a time in the history of America when the system had a slighter economic, political, and moral justification than in 1787. And yet with this real existence and growing evil before their

eyes, a bargain largely of dollars and cents was allowed to open the highway that led straight to the Civil War.

My position in this scholarly difference of opinion is with Dr. Du Bois rather than Dr. Jordan. I think that slavery could have been abolished at the time of the American Revolution. There are two traditional explanations or apologies for the failure of the founding fathers to do something about the institution of slavery.

The first explanation is that slavery was not then perceived as a problem—that it did not become a problem for men until the nineteenth century.

The second argument is almost the opposite. It says, yes, the founding fathers perceived slavery as a problem, but they believed it was on a natural course of extinction, withering of its own weight, dying of its own accord; and, therefore, no political or legislative steps were necessary.

Let us consider each of these justifications—first, the argument that slavery was not perceived as a problem. We can demonstrate the fallaciousness of this proposition by showing that, elsewhere in the civilized world at this time, other nations were taking steps against the institution of slavery. For example, in Great Britain, even before the American Revolution, a man named Granville Sharpe brought a legal case that challenged the institution of slavery—the so-called Somerset Case. Somerset was a man claimed as a slave by a West Indian merchant staying in Great Britain. And Sharpe, bringing the case into court, said on Somerset's behalf that when any human being steps onto the shores of Great Britain, he becomes free. That the air of England, as he put it in his brief, is too free for a man to be a slave here. Sharpe was upheld by the English court, and slavery was declared illegal within Great Britain (although not yet within the entire British Empire).

Then, shortly after the American Revolution, the French Empire experienced the great slave insurrection led by Toussaint l'Ouverture in Haiti in the 1790s. Soon after that, at the height of the French Revolution, the government abolished slavery throughout the empire, an action that, even though later reversed by Napoleon, showed that this was indeed a real problem for people in France, as well as people in England, at the time of the American Revolution.

And a third instance of action against slavery long before the American Civil War: Mexico and other Latin American countries freed themselves from Spain in the 1820s, and one of their first actions was to abolish slavery.

So we have strong argument against the proposition that slavery could not have been perceived as a problem by the American Revolutionaries. If that many other countries saw it as a problem at this time, why not the United States?

The second reason for believing that slavery was perceived as a problem, and therefore could have been abolished at the time of the American Revolution, is that although the new nation failed to act decisively against slavery, enough steps *were* taken to make it quite plain that slavery *was* recognized as a problem. These steps were of three kinds.

First, the Northern states, during and soon after the American Revolution, acted through state legislation to set in motion the abolition of slavery: Vermont, in its constitution of 1777; Massachusetts, in a series of legal cases in the early 1780s; Pennsylvania, Rhode Island, Connecticut, New York, and New Jersey, through state laws of 1780, 1784, 1799, 1804. The fact that these Northern states moved against slavery during this period suggests that the whole nation could have done so too.

Secondly, there was action against the slave trade, as distinct from slavery itself. In 1774, the first Continental Congress wrote as one of its resolutions: "We will neither import nor purchase any slave imported after the first day of December next, after which time we will wholly discontinue the slave trade and will neither be concerned in it ourselves nor will we hire our vessels nor sell our commodities or manufactures to those who are concerned in it." This, of course, was not lived up to. At the end of the American Revolution, the states of the Deep South, particularly South Carolina and Georgia, resumed the importation of slaves. But the fact that the Continental Congress had gone as far as it did, indicates that slavery was indeed perceived as a problem at that time.

And third and last, to demonstrate that slavery was perceived as a problem, laws were passed in a number of states of the Upper South—Virginia in 1782, Delaware in 1787, Maryland in 1790, Kentucky in 1798, Tennessee in 1801—to facilitate private manumission; that is, in contrast to the legislation of the Northern states to set Black people free, the Southern states passed laws making it possible for individual owners, if they wished, to free their slaves. Partly as a result of this legislation, the free Black population in Virginia grew from three thousand in 1780 to thirty thousand in 1810. But a law passed in Virginia in 1806 reversed this permissive legislation and made it more difficult for individual owners to set their slaves free.

Therefore, all this evidence, the action of the Northern states toward abolition, the first steps toward the abolition of the slave trade, the legislation in the Upper South for individual manumission indicates how seriously the problem of slavery was considered to be. As the historian Von Holtz put it, "but one more impulse" was needed to bring the institution to an end.

The second traditional apology for the inaction of the founding fathers is that they thought slavery was dying of its own accord. To defend this argument, three considerations are brought forward.

First, that slavery was abolished in the Northern states because it was unprofitable; second, that it was becoming unprofitable in the Upper South—for example, George Washington substituted wheat for tobacco in his Mount Vernon plantation, and slave labor was less suited to growing wheat than it was to tobacco. And, finally, that slavery would have become unprofitable in the Lower South as well had it not been for the invention of the cotton gin in the early 1790s, which the fathers could not have foreseen in 1776 or 1787.

I think this argument too is false. To say that slavery was abolished in the North because it was unprofitable runs against the evidence, collected by Dr. Zilversmitt in a recent study, that slave prices in the North remained high until the institution was abolished.

The argument that slavery was becoming unprofitable in the Upper South, as evidenced by George Washington's conversion to wheat, also does not hold water; for even if slavery in the Upper South was becoming unprofitable as a system of production, it remained profitable because slave-holders in Virginia and Maryland could sell their slaves to the producing plantations of the Lower South.

Therefore, the delegates, not only from the Deep South but from Virginia and Maryland as well, voted against that clause in the Northwest Ordinance proposed by Jefferson in 1784 which would have prohibited slavery in the territories of the West. George Mason told the Constitutional Convention in 1787 that unless slavery were quickly ended, the new states of the West would clamor for slaves, and the institution would go on increasing.

Finally, we move to the third contention—that slavery would have died in the states of the Lower South too had it not been for the invention of the cotton gin—and we must recognize that at the time of the Convention, South Carolina and Georgia did not feel slavery was unprofitable. Madison wrote to Thomas Jefferson, shortly after the close of the Convention, that South Carolina and Georgia had been inflexible on the point of slaves. The cotton gin did not revive slavery in the Lower South; as Professor Jordan puts it, "it whetted an existing appetite."

To sum up my response to these two traditional apologias for the inaction of the founding fathers: Slavery *was* perceived as a problem. It was morally condemned by the founding fathers. They took some steps, such as abolition in the Northern states, toward putting an end to slavery. They knew they had to take more. Further political action was necessary if the institution were to be destroyed, or even prevented from growing, and yet they did not take these steps.

Why was it that the drafters and signers of the Declaration of Independence and the Constitution failed to act?

I suggest three reasons: First is their solicitousness for private property. Slavery was, after all, a form of private property. And, in reading the debates of the Constitutional Convention, it is clear that one of the things that held back such a man as Gouverneur Morris, one of slavery's critics, was that he realized that to destroy chattel slavery in the South might call into question the justification of other forms of private property in the North. And therefore the Northern critics of slavery hesitated. And fear lest all private property be undermined was one reason the founding fathers failed to act.

A second equally important reason was prejudice. A man like Thomas Jefferson, who saw that slavery was wrong and worked to do something against slavery at many stages in his life, nevertheless was unable to imagine an America in which free Whites and free Blacks would live together as equals and fellow citizens. Jefferson's prejudice is most dramatically illustrated by the passage in his notes on Virginia written during the 1780s when he discussed the biological characteristics of Black men:

> Deep-rooted prejudices are entertained by the whites, ten thousand recollections of the blacks of the injuries they have sustained and there are the real distinctions which nature has made, which with many other circumstances will divide us into parties and produce convulsions which will probably never end but in the extermination of the one or the other race.
>
> To these objections which are political, there are others which are physical and moral. The first difference which strikes us is that of color and is this difference of no importance? Is it not the foundation of a greater or less share of beauty in the two races? Are not the fine mixtures of red and white, the expressions of every passion by greater or less suffusions of color in the one preferable to that eternal monotony which reigns in the countenances, that immovable veil of black which covers all the emotions of the other race?
>
> Add to these flowing hair, a more elegant symmetry of form, their own judgment in favor of the whites declared by their preference of them as uniformly as the preference of the orangutang for the black woman over those of his own species. The circumstance of superior beauty is thought worthy attention in the propagation of our horses, dogs and other domestic animals, why not in that of man? . . . Comparing them by their faculties of memory, reason, and imagination, it appears to me that in memory they are equal to the whites, in reason, much inferior, as I think one could scarcely be found capable of tracing and comprehending the investigations of Euclid. . . . And that in imagination they are dull, tasteless, and anomalous.

And Jefferson later stated that nothing is more certainly written in the book of fate than that these people should be free, but that nothing is also more certainly written than that Whites and Blacks cannot live together. This inability to imagine a society in which Blacks and Whites could live together held the founding fathers back from acting.

Finally, a third reason, in addition to property and to prejudice, is a certain passivity, a certain statesmanlike attitude, a certain pragmatism, a certain cool judiciousness in trying to see all sides of the question, which contrasts with the impulsive religiosity of the abolitionists in the nineteenth century.

Robert McColley, in his study on slavery in Jeffersonian Virginia, has contrasted in this way the different approach to the problem of slavery of the founding fathers, the statesmen of the American Revolution, and Quakers, religious enthusiasts like John Woolman:

> Not from the enlightened aristocrats, not from the fine theories of Republicanism and natural law, perhaps not even from the increased zeal for freedom fostered by the Revolution did the genuine spirit of emancipation derive. Instead, it came from the pious and primitive religious zeal of the dissenting sects, most notably the Quakers and the Methodists.

And he adds, further explicating this characteristic difference between the temper of the founding fathers and that of Quakers and other religious abolitionists,

> On point after point, the Quaker had faith in the power of moral energy to create the beneficial change, while the statesmen, supposedly some of the most liberal in American history, held to a gloomy set of immutable principles which man, it appeared, could have no power to alter.
>
> The statesmen believed that the Negroes must naturally be enemies to the whites. The Quakers held that the Negroes were capable of learning. The statesmen believed the intelligence of the Negro was inferior. The Quakers employed their meetinghouses for the evening instruction of slaves. The statesmen argued that emancipation must be accompanied by immediate removal and that a mongrelization of the races was to be feared. The Quakers held that emancipation must take precedence over any other consideration, and thus, that one more impulse was not forthcoming.

And the United States did not abolish slavery at the time of the American Revolution.

Exercises

Questions for Discussion

1. Why does Professor Lynd choose the time of the American Revolution as a logical time to assume that the question of slavery and its abolition should be raised? At what periods in their history was slavery abolished in certain other countries of the New World, for example, in Mexico?

2. What two reasons are usually advanced as to why slavery was not abolished at the time of the American Revolution?

3. What were the particulars of the Somerset Case? Why was it important?

4. What historical facts does Professor Lynd discuss which tend to indicate that slavery was perceived as a problem in eighteenth-century America?

5. What is meant by "manumission laws"? By "emancipation"? Explain the difference between the two. When and where do manumission laws begin to make their appearance? Does the trend continue, or is it reversed?

6. Both France and England abolished slavery in their colonies, yet the United States did not abolish it. In what way was the American case different from France and England? Other countries of the Western Hemisphere abolished slavery upon winning their independence, notably Mexico. In what way is the Mexican situation different from the American?

7. Respect for private property is one of the recurrent themes in the American ethic. How did the concept of private property enter into the arguments for and against slavery during the Constitutional Convention?

8. Explain the position of the Quakers regarding slavery. In what essential way was their attitude different from that of the statesmen?

9. Give briefly the three reasons which held the founding fathers from acting to abolish slavery.

10. What, in your opinion, could have been the reasons why slavery was declared illegal in England but not in the British Empire?

Activities

1. Have several class members analyze closely the passage quoted in this lesson from Thomas Jefferson's notes on Virginia and present their impressions and conclusions in the form of a panel discussion. Read that part of the notes from which the passage

is taken in order to put it into context. What is the theme and tone of the notes immediately before and after the segment quoted? The passage divides logically into two major sections. Where does the first end and the second begin? With what aspects of social intercourse do they each deal? Does Jefferson defend his value judgments with regard to skin color, hair quality and body shape on the basis of any inductive evidence? What psychological reasons—quite aside from the social status of one group with respect to the other—might there be for his conclusions? Are these same psychological factors potentially operative in the case of Blacks looking at Whites? What effect does the statement have on your image of Black people? What effect does it have on your image of *Jefferson*?

2. Read opinions of some additional historians, Black and White, as to why the United States did not abolish slavery at the time of the American Revolution. (Consult the bibliography for specific references. Perhaps the indices of these volumes can provide you with a page reference.) Among the White historians, note especially the regional Southern historians, such as C.Vann Woodward, W. J. Cash. Discuss the divergence of opinion on the basis of the author's race that Professor Lynd illustrates with one Black and White historian?

3. Read in some detail about the proceedings of the Constitutional Convention. Consider the arguments advanced on the question of slavery and its abolition. Keep in mind, as you read, the quotation from Professor Jordan: "During the post-war years . . . the Americans found that the philosophy of natural rights could not be made to serve as the cornerstone of effective government." And Professor Lynd's rejoinder "Could not or would not?"

4. Dr. Du Bois states: "There never was a time in the history of America when the system had a slighter economic, political, and moral justification than in 1787." Contrast this opinion with that of other historians, particularly those who view history largely from an economic approach. How many different textbook opinions can you find regarding the point at which slavery was least profitable in America? Keep in mind Professor Best's generalizations about the development and decline of the plantation economy, which you studied in an earlier lesson.

5. To what extent was slavery perceived as a problem by the men of the eighteenth century as compared to those of the nineteenth? One indication would be the extent to which it was publicly discussed in both eras and the detail in which the pros and cons were weighed. Consider the question from the purely economic point of view. Consider the detailed analysis given, for instance, by Frederick Law Olmsted, a Northern reporter who traveled through the slave states in the late 1850s (*The Slave States*, by Frederick Law Olmsted. Capricorn, G. P. Putnam's Sons, New York, 1959.) Note particularly his discussion on "The Cotton Kingdom." Do you find the question studied in such detail among any of the eighteenth century authors whom you've read?

Suggested Readings

The Negro in the American Revolution. By Benjamin Quarles. Chapel Hill Books, University of North Carolina Press, Chapel Hill, 1961. A detailed study of the part that Black people played in the important events relating to the American Revolution.

Black Heroes of the American Revolution, 1775–1783. Published by NAACP, New York, 1965. Short biographies of the main Black heroes of the American Revolution.

American Slavers and the Federal Law. 1837–1862. By Warren S. Howard. University of California Press, 1963. A study of the federal laws against the slave trade

History of the People of the United States: From the Revolution to Civil War. By Louis Filler. Noonday, New York, 1964.

Anti-Slavery and Reform Papers. By Henry David Thoreau. Harvest House, Montreal, 1963.

THE NORTHWEST ORDINANCE AND THE CONSTITUTIONAL CONVENTION

Staughton Lynd

In May, 1787, a national anti-slavery society was founded in England by Thomas Clarkson and other Englishmen. At the same time, in the United States, the Constitutional Convention assembled in Philadelphia. In July, 1787, the Constitutional Convention adopted the so-called "Three-Fifths Clause," which made slaves 60 percent human for purposes of political representation; but economically, they continued to be regarded as things.

And almost at the same day, ninety miles away in New York City, the Continental Congress passed the Northwest Ordinance, which banned slavery in the future states of Wisconsin, Michigan, Illinois, Indiana, and Ohio.

What is the meaning of these temporal coincidences? How can we explain the fact that the Constitution strengthened slavery, while the Northwest Ordinance appeared to move toward its abolition? What is the role of the United States Constitution in the history of the Afro-American? Or, as the Black abolitionist Frederick Douglass put it in his paper *The North Star* in 1849, "The Constitution of the United States, what is it? Who made it? For whom and for what was it made?"

To understand the problems that confronted the Continental Congress and the Constitutional Convention in 1787 and the manner in which they dealt with these problems through the compromises of the Constitution and the Northwest Ordinance, we must consider the geographical situation of the new nation as it stood in the late 1780s.

The Mississippi River marked the western boundary of the new nation, as set by the treaty with England in 1783. And the southern border stopped above Florida.

Only a part of this area, in 1787, had already been organized into states; portions of the land still constituted territory.

To the east of the crest of the Appalachian Mountains lie the original thirteen states. Eight of these, to the north—Massachusetts, Rhode Island, Connecticut, New Hampshire, New York, New Jersey, Pennsylvania, and Delaware—had abolished, or moved toward the abolition of, slavery by 1787. The slave states were Georgia, South Carolina, North Carolina, Virginia, and Maryland—the five states that were considered Southern States at the Constitutional Convention.

Between the Appalachians and the Mississippi River is a large area, part of the United States in 1787, but still politically in the form of territories not yet organized into states. This area was divided along the Ohio River; the five states north of the Ohio River —Wisconsin, Michigan, Illinois, Indiana and Ohio—were to become free states; the states south of the Ohio River were to become slave states.

The Northwest Ordinance of 1787, and the later Missouri Compromise, extended this line westward across the United States.

Now let us recapitulate those clauses of the United States Constitution that dealt directly with the institution of slavery.

Article One, Section Two, the so-called "Three-Fifths Clause," increased the political representation of the South in the House of Representatives by adding three-fifths of the slave population of the South to the White population of the South in determining the number of seats each state should have in Congress. This "Three-Fifths Clause," in effect, recognized the slaves as three-fifths of a human being. While increasing the political representation of his White masters, the Black was kept in economic slavery. This "Three-Fifths Clause" was the first and most significant compromise of the Constitutional Convention involving slavery.

Article One, Section Eight, empowered the United States government to assist the various states in putting down slave insurrections.

Article One, Section Nine, empowered the Congress, if it so wished, after a twenty-year period—that is, no earlier than 1807—to move to abolish the slave trade, although not the institution of slavery itself—a movement which, in fact, did take place in 1807.

Finally, Article Four, Section Two, the "Fugitive Slave Clause," without using the words *fugitive slave*, clearly states that the Northern States had an obligation to return fugitive slaves to their masters in the states of the South.

These four clauses had the effect of increasing, strengthening, and protecting the institution of slavery. Why did they come about?

Some of the reasons we considered in discussing the failure of the United States to abolish slavery at the time of the American Revolution. But still, in the specific situation of the Constitutional Convention—that summer of 1787 in Philadelphia—why did these compromises come about? And how can we explain the fact that, at the same time the Constitutional Convention in Philadelphia was strengthening slavery through these clauses, ninety miles away in New York, the Continental Congress was taking a step against slavery in the five future states of the Northwest?

First a note about the way historians have treated this problem. In discussions of the work of the Constitutional Convention until about the year 1900, it was generally assumed that resolving the conflict between North and South about slavery was one of the main tasks—if not *the* main task—of the Constitutional Convention. About 1900, however, it came to be believed that the conflict between North and South about slavery at the Convention had in fact been secondary. And it seems a plausible assumption that this neglect of slavery as an issue in the forming of the Constitution corresponded to the neglect of the Black man in the general policy of the United States during that period. This was the period of the passing of Jim Crow laws. This was the period of the disenfranchisement of the Black man in the Southern states. Only in our time, with the civil rights movement and the revival of interest in Afro-American history, have we again begun to appreciate the importance of sectional compromise based on slavery in the summer of 1787.

Let me emphasize that, in attempting to understand the part that slavery played in the work of the Constitutional Convention, we can't just read through Madison's minutes of the Convention and underline with our pencils every time the word *slave* or *slavery* is used. It's true that those words were used often. It's true that the South Carolina and Georgia delegates in particular were often on their feet saying that they would never give up their property in slaves.

But the influence of slavery on the work of the Constitutional Convention went far beyond explicit debate about whether slavery was right or wrong, explicit debate about whether or not to end the slave trade. Because the fact is that the sectional conflict at the Convention—the conflict between the five Southern states and the eight Northern ones—was based on the fact that slavery existed in the South and not in the North. As James Madison repeatedly stated at the Convention, "The institution of slavery and its consequences form the line of discrimination between the two contending groups" that have to compromise their differences. So that even when slavery was not discussed explicitly, even when the discussions seemed to be about the conflict between North and South, slavery, nonetheless, was there influencing the discussion.

This sectional conflict at the Convention, based on the existence or nonexistence of slavery in the contending states, went back much further than 1787. When Patrick Henry, in 1774, at the first Continental Congress, made his famous statement, "We are all American," he made it in the context of a debate as to whether slaves should be included in the basis of representation for delegates at the Congress. In 1783, the year the American Revolution ended, Thomas Jefferson, whom we don't ordinarily think of as a sectional statesman, wrote to the governor of Virginia that already dispute was raging in Congress as to whether Northern states or Southern states would first be added to the original thirteen. Already the sections were beginning to weigh their respective votes.

When, in the same year, 1783, the war ended, with the peace commissioners John Adams, Benjamin Franklin, and John Jay representing the interests of the United States in Europe, Southerners were quick to point out that these three men were Northerners who couldn't reliably be trusted to represent Southern interests. And Jefferson was named as Ambassador to France so that the South, too, would have a representative in Europe.

The point is that the sectional conflict based on slavery was not a new conflict, but one with which the Continental Congress had been struggling since its inception in 1774.

Now, given the fact that sectional conflict was already intense, and the South was already in a minority—a minority both in terms of the number of states that still kept the institution of slavery, and in terms of total population—why did the South consent to the United States Constitution? If the South already felt itself to be on the defensive, why did its delegates agree to sanction federal powers in 1787? Were Madison and Washington, as they steadfastly worked to strengthen the national government, traitors to the interests of their sections? Or was there some view of the future that nationalist Southerners then entertained that enabled them to be good Southerners and good nationalists at the same time?

Madison provides the clue. (Here I am paraphrasing.)
Madison saw that if the South were to agree in strengthening Congress, the plan which gave each state one vote would have to be changed in favor of the South. And in letters to Jefferson, to Ran-

dolph, and to Washington in the Spring of 1787, he foretold in a sentence the essential plot of the Convention drama. The basis of representation would be changed to allow representation by numbers as in the House of Representatives, as well as by state. Because a change was recommended to the Northern states by the actual superiority of their populousness. That is to say, the Northern delegates to the Constitutional Convention would favor a change from the basis of representation of one state, one vote to a basis of representation which created a House of Representatives based on population, because the North at the time of the Constitutional Convention had more people. But it would also be recommended to the Southern states, Madison insisted, because the Southerners expected to become more populous. And therefore the Southern delegates could agree to strengthening the national government, because they expected as their numbers increased to dominate it.

Over and over again members of the Convention stated as something on which all agreed that as soon as the Southern and Western populations should predominate, which must happen in a few years, the South would be compensated for any advantages wrung from it by the North in the meantime.

"He must be short-sighted, indeed," declared King on July 12, "who does not foresee that whenever the Southern states shall be more numerous than the Northern, they can and will hold a language that will awe the Northern states into justice. If they threaten to separate now in case injury shall be done them, will their threats be less urgent or effectual when force shall back their demands?" "It has been said," Gouverneur Morris added, "that North Carolina, South Carolina, and Georgia only will in a little time have a majority of the people of America. They must in that case include the great interior country. And everything was to be apprehended from their getting the power into their hands."

Thus, in James Madison's opinion and also in mine, this was the basis of the Convention compromises. The North agreed to strengthening the national government, because the North had a present majority in population. The South agreed to strengthening the national government because the South expected to have a majority in population. And the specific compromises over slavery—the "Three-Fifths" compromise, the compromise over the slave trade, the "Fugitive Slave Clause," and the clause giving the federal government the power to put down insurrections—reflected this larger sectional compromise between the North and the South.

This gives us a rough idea, at least, of the dynamics of the Constitutional Convention. Why is it that, at the same time, as part of the Constitutional compromise, the North appeared to give in to the South so much at the Constitutional Convention in Philadelphia while at the same time, at the Continental Congress, the Northwest Ordinance was passed abolishing slavery in the future states of

Wisconsin, Michigan, Illinois, Indiana, and Ohio? And the Southern delegates at that Continental Congress voted for the Northwest Ordinance. Why?

Let me suggest three reasons. The first reason was that, although today we think that these five states of the Northwest would have automatically become free states, that was by no means so clear in 1787. The great wave of population over the Appalachians at that time was coming from Virginia and North Carolina into the future states of Kentucky and Tennessee. Southerners expected that that wave of population, carrying, for example, the families of Abraham Lincoln and Jefferson Davis, would also sweep northward over the Ohio into the states of Ohio, Indiana, and Illinois, so that these states might very well vote with the South rather than the North. And, in fact, although that expectation failed to materialize, it was not an irrational one. The southern portions of these states contain many Southerners; and there was a distinct battle in Illinois, for example, in the 1820s, as to whether or not the Northwest Ordinance would be repealed because of the interests of this Southern population. So, one reason why the South voted for the Northwest Ordinance was that it thought that these Northwest states might actually add votes to the Southern interests in Congress.

A second reason: Until 1787, the Continental Congress had been struggling to legislate for the western territories as a whole. It had not yet drawn the line along the Ohio River between the Northwest territories and the Southwest territories. But what it did, in 1787, was to say that these states will be free; and we can plausibly speculate that this also meant to Southerners that the states of the Southwest would be slave. And when, in fact, they applied for admission, a few years later, Northerners accepted their admission as slave states, as if tacitly recognizing that a bargain had been struck in 1787.

A third reason that Southerners voted for the Northwest Ordinance, despite the fact that it abolished slavery, was that a clause in the Northwest Ordinance lowered the population size required for admission to the Union; so that the South, expecting those states to vote with the South when they entered Congress, and because it seemed that their admission would occur soon, was the more prepared to support the ordinance.

And so, summing up the relationship between the Northwest Ordinance and the Constitutional Convention, and the apparently contradictory fact that the Constitution strengthened slavery while the Northwest Ordinance weakened it, we can say, I think, as follows: The evidence suggests that the motives which moved men in making the Ordinance and in making the Constitution were essentially the same. Southerners who sought to guarantee slave property and to make possible a stronger Southern voice in Congress saw the Northwest settlement, even without slavery, as a means to these ends.

At the Convention, sanctions for slavery—the "Three-Fifths Clause" and the slave-trade clause—seemed necessary to bring about the same result: Protection against emancipation, and a Southern majority in the House. In each case, the North made the compromises the South demanded. But in Congress, because of the South's mistaken assumptions about the future of the Northwest, an antislavery clause could be included. The "Fugitive-Slave Clause," adopted unanimously by both bodies, shows, if not that there was a sectional compromise between the Congress and the Convention, at least that the makers of both the Northwest Ordinance and the United States Constitution were ready to compromise the concept that all men are equal. This was the fundamental compromise that occurred in both bodies in 1787.

We have seen some coincidences of the year 1787. Now consider some of them of the year 1800, which made plain the significance of the compromises of the Constitution and the Northwest Ordinance.

In 1800, a slaveholder, Thomas Jefferson, was elected President. He would have lost to his Northern opponent, John Adams, had not the "Three-Fifths Clause," written by the Constitutional Convention, strengthened the South in the Electoral College. And Jefferson, of course, went on to acquire the Louisana Purchase, to open it to slavery, and thus to smooth the path of the "peculiar institution" west of the Mississippi River.

In 1800, France and England temporarily adjourned the Napoleonic Wars to attempt to destroy a man they regarded as their common enemy: the Haitian revolutionary Toussaint l'Ouverture.

In 1800, Gabriel Prosser led the first large American slave insurrection. The rebels carried a flag which said, "Death or Liberty." But the governor of Virginia, James Monroe, executed the rebel slaves.

The year 1800 showed that the nineteenth century would not be a good one for the Black man in America.

Exercises

Questions for Discussion

1. What is the so-called three-fifths clause? What was its purpose? What was its effect?

2. Describe the functions of the Constitutional Convention and the Continental Congress.

3. What were the boundaries of the United States as of 1787? What portion of it had not as yet been organized into states? Of that portion organized into states, which were slave states and which were free states?

4. What did the Northwest Ordinance establish?

5. What, although not definitely stated, was implied by the Northwest Ordinance?

6. Why did the South agree to the terms of the Northwest Ordinance? Why did the North?

7. What important historical consequences did the three-fifths clause produce thirteen years after its adoption?

8. In addition to the three-fifths clause, name three other compromises which the Constitutional Convention made involving slavery.

9. Name one or two manifestations of North-South regionalism that became evident at the time of the peace treaty with England? (That is, at the moment when the United States' destiny as a nation seemed assured.) To what do you attribute these manifestations?

10. What assumptions on the part of the Southern delegates prompted them to disregard their minority status and agree to a strong national government? To agree to representation by numbers in the House of Representatives?

Activities

1. Dr. Lynd mentions a National Anti-Slavery Society founded in England by Thomas Clarkson. Do some research on this (or similar) societies. In what geographical areas did it concentrate its efforts? Were the founders swayed primarily by religious, political, or economic motives? Did it form the model for other such societies?

2. Read through Madison's minutes of the Constitutional Convention. Notice the fever with which regional ideals are upheld. Does slavery seem to be regarded as a moral issue or as an accomplished fact that has to be dealt with as smoothly as possible?

3. Do some research on the election of 1800. What were the chances, by estimates of contemporary witnesses, of the two men, Adams and Jefferson? Were there any grumblings from the North as a result of Jefferson's artificial victory?

4. One gets the impression that the North-South regionalism, as evidenced at the inception of statehood, had already gone beyond the stage of the political desire for power, and represented two different ways of life and perhaps the potential for two distinct cultures. In your opinion, can we view Northern and Southern America as culturally distinct? As one means of substantiating

your position, compare illustrations of the period which depict modes of dress, types of dwelling, occupations, recreations, social stratification, and so forth, in the North and in the South. Have you found, in your readings, any mention of the distinctive difference in speech habits which we associate with the North and with the South? Do you attribute a major role to the difference in topography and climate? Or was this simply one of many factors to be considered?

5. Locate an account of the debate at the first Continental Congress (1774) during which Patrick Henry made his "We are all American" statement. Pay particular attention to the dual way slaves are regarded (as property and as men) by the delegates. Is there any debate around incorporating the institution of slavery as a permanent feature of the new nation?

Suggested Readings

The Anti-Slavery Vanguard. By Martin Duberman. Princeton University Press, Princeton, N.J., 1965. Essays on the Abolitionists and their effect on the slavery issue.

The British Anti-Slavery Movement. By Sir Reginald Coupland. Frank Cass and Co., Ltd.,London, 1964. A concise history of the British Anti-Slavery Movement, with a new introduction by J. D. Fage.

The Abolitionists. By Louis Richames. Putnam, New York, 1963. A comprehensive view of the Abolitionist Movement and the men who made it a great force against slavery.

Black Abolitionists. By Benjamin Quarles. Oxford University Press, New York, 1969. The first book that is devoted solely to the role of the Black Abolitionists. A useful and long awaited study.

They Came in Chains. By Saunders Redding. Lippincott, Philadelphia, 1950. A general history of the Black Americans.

SLAVERY AND BLACK AMERICA

Sterling Stuckey

Black people who came to the New World did not come from
societies barren of culture and achievement. In fact, they came from
complex societies in which religious, political, economic, and artistic
development had reached a high level. It would be difficult to imagine
the degree of anguish, of suffering, of hardship which the slave trade
and slavery caused these Africans. From our studies of the past we
know that they were torn from their tribal moorings, forced to make
the march from the interior to the shores of the Atlantic, branded,
and made to undergo the additional horrors of begin stuffed into
ships and forced to cross the ocean under the most inhuman circumstances.

When they arrived in the New World, Africans were made to
undergo the process of "seasoning" with its unbelievable cruelty. This
activity was designed to make them servile dependents, to break the
hold which Africa held over her scattered children. It was the
application of violence and psychological warfare—especially in the
West Indies and in North America—with a view toward destroying

Overseers usually managed operations on plantations. Most overseers appointed carefully screened blacks to be drivers; thus,
these blacks became instrumental in the plantation power structure. Often the inhumane treatment and punishment which was
ordered by the overseer, was executed by the black drivers, under
vigilant eye.   (*Library of Congress*)

beliefs and behavior a thousand years in the shaping. Owing to the far reaching impact of the cultural imperialism involved, this process was more than a founding stone on which the subjugation of slaves was based; it bears a direct relationship to the current oppression of Black people in the West.

The psychological war against Black people, designed to cripple them culturally in order to more effectively control them physically, received fulsome support from the judicial system of North America. The movements of slaves were severely restricted: they could be challenged by any white person and made to produce a pass; they could not make contracts; they could not own property; they could not marry; they could not, except in rare instances, receive an education. It was also a "crime" for a slave to defend himself against attacks from Whites; it was a crime to meet in groups (usually exceeding three people) unless a White person was present. As slavery became a fully developed institution during the nineteenth century, slave codes were strengthened, and slaveholders became increasingly hostile to associations between free and enslaved blacks. That was, in brief, the "law and order" of the slave codes, of the white man's legal system, sanctioned by church and state and family—by lawyers, preachers, politicians, professors—sanctioned by the American "democracy."

Professor Kenneth Stampp, in his brilliant *The Peculiar Institution*, has presented the five basic steps employed by numerous masters in seeking to make a "good" slave: to maintain strict discipline, to implant in the slave a sense of inferiority born of his African ancestory, to awe the slave with a sense of the power of White people, to train the slave to believe that his interest and that of the master are one and the same, and to instill in the slave a sense of his helplessness.

Although slave codes could be enforced rather effectively on large plantations, Richard Wade has pointed out that it was much more difficult to control slaves in cities. This was partly because there were free Blacks in cities; the knowledge that some Black people were free might embolden the enslaved. Moreover, slaves in cities usually did not live in or even near the master's residence; they were able to live apart from the master and to enjoy a measure of privacy. Slaves in cities were also permitted to hire themselves out, to earn a little money with which, if enough could be amassed, they might eventually purchase their freedom. Between 1830 and 1860, however, opportunities for purchasing freedom were less prevalent as sectional strife mounted and the South became increasingly paranoid.

Were slaves insensitive to their suffering and that of others as some White historians contend? Slavery was not an unrecorded experience and slaves were not silent on this point. Sojourner Truth's mother, for example, spoke for most Black women when she related, as Sojourner sat at her feet, the grief slavery had visited upon her,

"After the Sale! Slaves Going South from Richmond," a painting by Eyre Crowe, 1853. Richmond became one of the main Southern cities in the ghastly slave-dealing business.   (*Courtesy Chicago Historical Society*)

separating her from her children. This grief was known by Sojourner years later when her son was taken from her, causing her to remark that she felt "as mighty as a nation," as "tall as the world," and determined to somehow recover him. Yet it is not possible for us ever to know the full extent of the heartache which slavery caused Black people. Frederick Douglass has captured much of the pain and pathos of Black mothers:

> The hearth is desolate. The unconscious children who once sang and danced in her presence are gone. She gropes her way, in the darkness of age, for a drink of water . . . the grave is at the door, and now . . . this most needed time for the exercise of that tenderness and affection which children only can bestow on a declining parent—my poor old grandmother, the devoted mother of twelve children, is left all alone, in yonder little hut, before a few dim cinders.

Even though slavery did not recognize Black marriages or Black families, Black people, far more than sociologists and historians would have us believe, managed to display a humanity toward each other that has yet to be recognized by most scholars. The evidence is not only found in Douglass and Truth and Solomon Northrop and those other individuals who put their thoughts down on paper or in song. No less revealingly, it is found in the actions of the thousands of Black people who, as slavery came to an end, searched for relatives and friends from whom they had long been separated. As Lerone Bennett has demonstrated, there was no small measure of solidarity among ex-slaves during the period following slavery, the Reconstruction period. The basis for this solidarity was rooted in the ante-bellum period.

For the more than two hundred years of slavery White America made life practically unbearable for the millions of slaves who did America's dirty work, whose gift of muscle did so much to build the country, to transform a wilderness. Black people were treated, in many instances, as mere things—to be used and driven until they were no longer, like Douglass' grandmother, worth using. It is no exaggeration to say that White America tried to rob Black people of their very humanity, to kill their spirits.

Black people resisted with the few tools at their command. There were countless individual attacks on White people. There were slave revolts. And there were acts of "day to day resistance"—feigning illness, sabotage, malingering, and self-mutilation, among others. But the power of whites was usually unassailable and crushing in its impact, and countless Blacks were broken by slavery.

What were the circumstances and the values which sustained Black people during the terrible ordeal of slavery? Did they somehow manage a degree of control over the shaping of values? Did large numbers develop a world within a world with values more congenial to their own needs? No historian has given full-length treatment to the question of the existence of a subterranean slave world, but a few have provided interesting leads, especially in the areas of music and religion. We now know that the music and folktales of the slave were very much influenced by Africa, and that the religion of slaves was also under some significant African influence; these considerations, in combination with New World experiences, account for the differences between Black and White art and religion today and for differences in the ways in which very large numbers within the two groups perceive America and the world.

Dr. Du Bois has argued that for two centuries slaves in North America regarded themselves as Africans. Though he is probably somewhat wide of the mark, he is closer to the truth on this point than other scholars, who delight in dismissing the view that slaves were significantly influenced by Africa. Du Bois' position is worthy of very serious consideration, for we know that free Blacks in the North for more than two hundred years referred to themselves either as Africans or as "free Africans." Moreover, they placed the word African in the names of their organizations and displayed, in important instances, keen interest in Africa. In addition, some slaves as late as 1816 were referring to themselves as Africans, as the activities of Vesey and his slave associates demontrate. Clearly there is need for further research in this area.

Not unrelated to this African consciousness is the fact that, in addition to looking for relatives when slavery came to an end, not a few Black people began ridding themselves of names given by slave masters. And just as numerous Blacks communicate with each other today in ways that are largely foreign to most Whites, so too did they do this—probably a great deal more—during slavery. In this regard, Booker Washington's account of the slave's communications system in *Up From Slavery* is very suggestive.

When the institution of slavery finally ceased to exist, racism hung like an incubus over White Americans, causing most to persist in regarding Black people as objects to be used and exploited on all levels of contact, whether in education or in politics, in economics or in art, in "freedom" as in slavery. (Black people had also become, for White America, the very essence of evil and eroticism—the incarnation, as James Baldwin has observed, of all of the things which White Americans felt and feared in themselves.)

This attitude of ownership, of holding an almost divine right over the destinies of Black people, seemed to have become deeply rooted in White American consciousness. Its practical effects would be felt a century following slavery in the White American's attitude toward education for Blacks (they insist upon White control over Black education), toward Black political participation (Blacks play practically no role whatever in the formulation of laws by which White America

94

A scene from a painting by Thomas S. Noble, "Last Sale of Slaves on Courthouse Steps" in St. Louis, 1860.   (*Missouri Historical Society*)

insists they must live), toward the role of Blacks in the economy of the country (those who were denied an economic base following slavery would, a century hence, be dependent in almost every way on White economic good will—despite the centuries of forced labor given), and toward Black people in almost every important theater of life. In fact, most White Americans seem to believe sincerely that Americans—White ones—are better than other people, that the "lives of American boys," that is, White boys, are more valuable than the lives they are taking in other countries—and in America. This, of course, is a species of madness, one which is in large part related to the slave era and to the genocidal aggression practiced against the Indians.

With respect to the legacy of slavery, John Dollard's *Caste & Class in a Southern Town* has provided a significant conceptual approach to viewing the exploitation of Blacks by Whites. Dollard refers to the "gains" of segregation, that is, to how White people benefit from such an arrangement. While it is true that his theoretical framework was not comprehensive enough, that it might have been stronger, he did focus on the economic, social, and sexual gains of White Southerners, gains which have made it extremely difficult indeed for Southern Whites to give up their racism. (These gains, especially the economic and social, also operate very strongly against Northern Whites giving up racism.) But what Dollard and other social scientists failed to understand is that Black people, following slavery, were plunged into a status which was worse than that of colonial subjects. With true liberation, even during Reconstruction, a remote possibility, and with facing an antagonist who could only be moved by force or by severe, dramatic instances of bloodletting (and then only temporarily), Blacks for more than a century would win meager victories at the cost of great suffering. The "American way" of social change, which had won very substantial victories for immigrant groups, would have little relevance indeed for Black people for reasons attributable very largely to what slavery had made of the country.

The experiences through which Black people went during slavery, the systematic and sustained victimization savagely applied, were probably unparalleled in all of modern and most of ancient history. That they fight at all, as Ronald Fair has said, is itself a victory. That they survived to take the lead in their struggle is, as Ralph Ellison has written, one of the great triumphs of the human spirit in the history of the world. But what is more important than those considerations—and profoundly relevant to the possibility of a future for the world—is the need for a major exploration of what slavery did to the institutions and personalities of American White people. The results of that investigation might help mankind cure the sickness which is threatening life on this planet.

This group of Africans (with numerous emaciated children) was abducted from a slave ship by British seamen, subsequent to Britain's abolition of the slave trade. (*Library of Congress*)

Exercises

Questions for Discussion

1. List two activities which slaves were not permitted to engage in.

2. What is the historical basis for the feeling among Whites of ownership which has become deeply rooted in White American consciousness?

3. During the nineteenth century, with the increasingly punitive nature of the slave codes, what actions by slaves were considered crimes?

4. What, according to Professor Stampp were the five essential steps taken to control the slaves? In your opinion, was any one step more crucial than the other?

5. One of Professor Stampp's steps recalls the words of Professor Best: ". . . the internal stability of the plantation and therefore the society as a whole requires a convergence between the values of the slaves or indentured workers and the actual behavior demanded of them in the process of production." Discuss in what ways the two men's views coincide. Is there a difference in emphasis? Point of departure?

6. Go back and read through the five steps. Substitute the word "White" everywhere you see the word "master" and the word "Black" everywhere you see the word "slave" or "bondsman." Dr. Stampp's formula generalizes only with reference to a specific historical period. Does your substitution of words which do not point to specific historically observed relationships lengthen the historical period for which the generalization remains valid? shorten it? change it? Does Mr. Stuckey choose his analogies from any specific historical period(s)? How do you know? Name two dates as approximate beginning and ending dates for the period to which Mr. Stuckey is referring.

7. Why was it more difficult to control the slaves in cities?

8. What were some ways in which slaves in America managed to retain some sense of an African identity?

9. What were some ways—which became evident at the time of emancipation—in which Black people had striven to preserve an identity, a sense of self and of ties with each other as Blacks? Is there any specific example for which you can find a parallel in the present-day efforts to retain and more fully recapture a Black identity?

10. What is meant in this lesson by "subterranean life"? What are some evidences by which we know of its existence?

1. Read some of the stories collected by the folklorist Zora Neale Hurston (for instance, in her volume *Mules and Men*, 1935). Keep in mind Mr. Stuckey's words: "What Miss Hurston is suggesting is that Black slaves . . . had to devise certain ways to survive. But they were not committed, spiritually and psychologically, to these attitudes." Can you infer this at all from the implications in the tales?

2. Do some research on Henry Highland Garnet and David Walker. What were the accomplishments of each? What do they share in common? In what ways do their lives and activities illustrate a community life and a particular method of communication?

3. Read carefully in Booker T. Washington's book, *Up From Slavery*, that section to which Mr. Stuckey refers that deals with the conscious accepting or rejecting of the master's name and the choosing of one's own. Can you find similar accounts in other Black writers who witnessed the period following emancipation? Compare this with the methods employed by certain groups of Black people today (the Muslims, followers of Elijah Mohammed; the members of the New York-based Yoruba Temple Group). What images of themselves are radiated by people who thus rename themselves for philosophical reasons? Are there parallels among these various groups?

4. The five steps to which Mr. Stuckey refers have been presented to you in an abstract, general form. Imagine you are a slave, undergoing indoctrination into the system through these five steps. Give specific activities and circumstances into which you are drawn which reflect these successive stages in your life.

5. Imagine you are a slave owner. How would you go about effecting the change in your slaves? Would the number of slaves you had, your degree of prominence in the community, the type of crop you plant, affect your procedure? Are you entirely conscious of what you are doing? What role, direct and indirect, do non-slaveholding white and poor whites play in the successful completion of each step?

Suggested Readings

The Peculiar Institution. By Kenneth M. Stampp. Vintage Book, Random House, New York, 1964.

Up From Slavery. By Booker T. Washington.   Dell, New York, 1965. Autobiography of a former slave who became a great educator.

The First Emancipation. By Arthur Zilversmit. A book about a little known aspect of slavery in America.

White Over Black. By Winthrop D. Jordan. The University of North Carolina Press, Chapel Hill, 1968. A massive book about American attitudes toward Black people.

The Right of Revolution. By Truman Nelson. Beacon Press, Boston, 1968. A defense of the rights to revolt.

SLAVERY AND WHITE AMERICA

Sterling Stuckey

In considering the relationship between slavery and American society and between those who were enslaved and those who plunged them into this dreadful state, it is well to recall that the "fathers" of the Republic, the American philosophers of "freedom" and "democracy," Thomas Jefferson and George Washington, *were themselves slaveholders*. Unwilling to abolish the barbarism that was slavery, Jefferson, Washington, and others of great stature gave their approval to the birth of a nation which held hundreds of thousands of people in captivity. Thus freedom and slavery were joined in unholy and unwholesome wedlock. Never in the annals of history had a people formed a nation under more hypocritical circumstances. (Do not forget that before the White man came to these shores the land belonged to the Indians. Recall that the Indians, at the moment of the birth of the nation, were being systematically slaughtered and removed from their land. Remember that the Indians—the people who had for centuries owned the land—were being called "savages" by those who were killing and robbing and scalping them.)

Fully a century before the founding fathers made their profound and far-reaching compromises, their ancestors, from roughly 1619 to 1660, had wrestled with the problem of how best to exploit the labor of Black people. They decided that enslavement for life, rather than work for a specified period of time, would be the solution. Christianity was used to justify the bondage of the deeply religious African people who were forcibly brought to America. Thus the church became one of the first American institutions to give its blessings (and those of its White God) to the enslavement of Black people. The political leaders in time established by law the enslavement that was already in effect by custom and that some would later claim was brought on by "economic necessity." But the only necessity, if there was one at all, was the seeming inner compulsion of some White Americans to use others in order to gain a life of relative ease for themselves.

By the time of the American revolution, vital institutions in American society—religious, educational, political, economic, legal, and social—were feeding the engine of slavery and feeding the sickness which enabled White America to establish slavery in the first place. The rhetoric of the revolutionary period, despite the subsequent elimination of slavery in the North, deepened contradictions, establishing a split in the mind which enabled most White people to declare the country free and the people free despite the existence in their midst of perhaps the most fiendish system of slavery in the history of man. In the face of destruction directed at Indians and attempts to rob Black people of their humanity, the constant refrains of freedom were to echo down through the generations as part of the oral and written history of the country. Carried in countless political speeches by officials on all levels of American society, the fantasy of freedom was driven deep into the psyches of White Americans. Racism—the belief that a people because of the color of their skin are superior to those of a different color and therefore are justified, through manipulation and control of the power at their disposal, in having superior economic, social, and political positions—very early became the key reality of American life, shaping the way large numbers of White people looked out at the world and in toward themselves, laying the foundations for the later far-flung life-destroying practices of America vis-à-vis people of color. So strong was the feeling among the great mass of White people that they were superior to Blacks, that the schism in their minds—preaching freedom in the midst of slavery—caused relatively little pain and comparatively few real misgivings.

The process by which racism was transmitted from generation to generation during slavery has yet to be seriously examined. The subordinate position of Black people, who were held down by brute force and psychological warfare, has not been examined in all of its ramifications, though Kenneth Stampp has done a superb job of exploring

102

RAFFLE

Mr. Joseph Jennings respectfully informs his friends and the public that, at the request of many acquaintances, he has been induced to purchase from Mr. Osborne, of Missouri, the celebrated

DARK BAY HORSE, "STAR,"

Aged five years, square trotter and warranted sound; with a new light Trotting Buggy and Harness; also, the dark, stout

MULATTO GIRL, "SARAH,"

Aged about twenty years, general house servant, valued at *nine hundred dollars*, and guaranteed, and

Will be Raffled for

At 4 o'clock P. M., February first, at the selection hotel of the subscribers. The above is as represented and these persons who may wish to engage in the usual practice of raffling, will, I assure them, be perfectly satisfied with their destiny in this affair.

The whole is valued at its just worth, fifteen hundred dollars; fifteen hundred

CHANCES AT ONE DOLLAR EACH.

The Raffle will be conducted by gentlemen selected by the interested subscribers present. Five numbers will be allowed to complete the Raffle. BOTH OF THE ABOVE DESCRIBED CAN BE SEEN AT MY STORE, No. 78 Common St., second door from Camp, at from 9 o'clock A. M. to 3 P. M.

Highest throw to take the first choice; the lowest throw their remaining prize, and the fortunate winners will pay twenty dollars each for the refreshments furnished on the occasion.

N. B. No chances recognized unless paid for previous to the commencement.

J⸰SEPH JENNINGS.

Since slaving was such a prime enterprise, advertisements of this sort were not the least bit unusual. (*Frederic Lewis, Inc.*)

An advertisement of skilled workers with notations of estimated financial values. (*Ohio Historical Society Library*)

56 VERY CHOICE
Cotton Plantation SLAVES,
MECHANICS,
SEAMSTRESSES, COOKS, &C.

By J. A. BEARD & MAY.   J. A. BEARD, Auctioneer.

WILL BE SOLD AT AUCTION,
ON MONDAY, JANUARY 29, 1855,
At 12 o'Clock, at Banks' Arcade,
WITHOUT RESERVE,

The following list of Choice and Valuable SLAVES, from the Plantation of Gen. W. BAILEY, Lake Providence, La., viz:

ONE FAMILY.

1.—BIG HENRY, aged about 21 years, a superior field hand, fine servant, and first rate cotton picker; and his wife—

2.—AMY, aged about 18, superior cotton picker and fine servant.

3—LITTLE HENRY, aged about 16, slightly near-sighted, a superior cotton picker and fine servant.

ONE FAMILY.

4.—BONTON, aged about 26 years, a complete ostler and field hand, and superior cotton picker, and an invaluable servant.

5.—LITTLE MILLY, his wife, aged about 19, a superior cotton picker, and a most valuable hand.

ONE FAMILY.

6.—STEPHEN, aged about 24 years, a fine ox driver and superior cotton picker, etc.

7.—BIG FANNY, aged about 24, his wife, a good seamstress, and superior cotton picker and field hand; his child—

8.—WIRT HENRY, aged about 20 months.

ONE FAMILY.

9.—CASWELL, ox driver, aged about 30, very slightly ruptured, a fine field hand, and an invaluable servant.

10.—AGGY, his wife, aged about 80, a superior cook, washer and ironer, a most valuable woman, and superior field hand and cotton picker.

11.—FAYETTE HENRY, her child, aged about 5 —

12.—STANHOPE McLANHAN —

ONE FA[MILY.]

13.—BIG JIM, a rough carpenter, [ ] field hand and cotton picker, aged about 2[ ] or 26 years—invaluable.

14.—ANN RANDOLPH, his wife, aged about 22 years, can [ ]ck cotton with any negro, and is invaluable.

ONE FAMILY.

[ ]ORGE, aged about 26 years, plain but useful planta[ti]on smith, a fine driver, and one of the best cotto[n] [pi]ckers and field hands in the State, without exceptio[n]

[LI]TTLE FANNY, his wife, aged about 23 years, [a] most valuable cotton picker and field hand.

17.—RODERICK DHU, her child, aged about 4 years. This man and wife can pick more cotton than any two [ ] hands in the State.

ONE FAMILY.

18.—PETER, aged about 47, carpenter and cooper, a trusty and valuable servant, (formerly servant of Thomas Jefferson); can build a house out and out.

19.—HARRIET, his wife, aged about 22 years, a most [supe]rior cotton picker, and invaluable.

20.—THOMAS JEFFERSON, their child, aged about 3

ONE FAMILY.

21.—JACK, aged about 49 or 50, one of the best drive[rs] the State, and invaluable.

22.—DOLL[Y,] his wife, aged about 21 years; can pick from 420 to 500 lbs. of cotton per day; a superior field hand, sews well.

23.—NELSON, aged about 28, slightly ruptured; a most valuable field hand and superior cotton picker; has never lost an hour's work from his rupture.

24.—JORDEN, aged about 19, a very valuable field hand, a fine cotton picker and ginner.

25.—ADDISON, aged about 18, an invaluable field hand and cotton picker, one of the best.

26.—SAM, aged about 18, a fine cotton picker, and as valuable a boy as can be found.

27.—WASHINGTON, aged about 15 or 16, a fine cotton picker and valuable boy.

28.—DICK, aged about 20, a fine cotton picker and superior gin hand.

29.—CHARLES, aged about 16, field hand, a good boy.

30.—JOHN, aged about 28 years, fine cotton picker and field hand.

ONE FAMILY.

31.—EDWARD, aged about 19, one amongst the best cotton pickers and field hands in the State.

32.—MARGARET, his wife, aged about 18, a valuable cotton picker; and her two children—

33 and 34.—JENNY LIND, aged 2 years, and Infant 3 mos.

[ ]—BIG WILLIAM, aged about 20, a fine cotton picker and good servant—a strong and valuable man.

[ ]M HENRY, aged about 19 years, a fine field hand and [ ]er.

[ ] or 12 years, cotton picker, etc.

[ ]about 14 years, fine cotton picker, etc.

ON[E FAMILY.]

39.—JESSEE, aged about 2[ ] fine fiel[d hand,] pick 500 cotton; invaluable boy.

[ ]—CAROLINE, his wife, aged 17 years, can [ ] as Jessee.

[ ]—AMANDA, aged about 18, fine field hand, etc.

[ ]—MARY PATE, aged about 18, field hand and cotton picker, etc.

[ ]—YELLOW MARY, aged about 18, a good seamstress, can pick 500 lbs. cotton per day.

44—DINAH, aged about 45, a good field hand, strong and valuable; can pick 350 lbs. cotton; good midwife.

45.—PHILLIS, aged 20, field hand and cotton picker.

46.—NANCY, aged 17,   do.

47.—MARY CASWELL, aged 12, field h'd and cotton picker.

48.—SUCKEY, aged about 11 or 12,   do.   do.

49.—BETSY, aged 11,   do.   do.

50.—SALLY, aged 11, orphan,   do.   do.

51.—NELLY, aged 52, midwife, etc., good hand to give medicine, and take care of children.

52.—JANE, aged 18, fine cotton picker, and invaluable.

TERMS OF SALE, CASH, or on a credi[t], on approved notes or drafts, with such interest as may be agreed on between vendor and purchaser. *Acts of Sale before T. O. Stark, Not. Pub., at the expense of the purchasers* certain of its aspects. But an array of institutions, public and private, were mobilized in slavery on a scale tantamount to preparation for war in order to coerce and "persuade" Black people into satisfying the greed, the lusts—in a word, the twisted desires—of their slave overlords. Thus the "freedom" of the founders and their followers, a concept which had developed out of the spirit of the Renaissance, was, as Du Bois has observed, "the freedom to destroy freedom," the freedom to become the masters of men, the freedom to imprison one-self in a complex web of self-deluding lies, the freedom to become bearers of death and enslavement to much of the world.

The enslavement of Blacks, the failure to eradicate the evil that was slavery, opened the gates of the country to successive waves of immigrants who felt, not unnaturally, no greater responsibility to live out the democratic rhetoric of the country than any other Whites in America. Indeed, as Professor John Hope Franklin has remarked, the failure of the founders of the country to eliminate slavery meant that they could not go to the gates of the country and say: "this (freedom) is what we fought and died for; this is what we stand on; if you cannot subscribe to our belief in freedom for all men, you cannot enter."

Most White people saw the source of the racial problem in Black people, not in themselves and their institutions. Black people were the dark repositories into which White people attempted to project their fears and unload their phobias. Poet and critic Sterling Brown has dealt with White stereotypes more brilliantly than any other author. More than thirty years ago, in "Negro Character As Seen by White Authors," Brown exposed to view stereotypes that were the common property of very large segments of White America. His very suggestive work in this field has yet to be utilized by historians.

The victims of one of the most sustained and comprehensive cam-paigns of sexual aggression in the history of the world, Blacks were labeled promiscuous and sexually base. The victims of the most heinous acts of violence, Black people would later find themselves, in the White American mind, transformed into "brutes." Subjected to the "law and order" of the slave codes, Blacks who did not conform were, interestingly enough, considered lawless and unruly. (Indeed, U. B. Phillips later had the temerity and the imagination to entitle one of his chapters on slavery "Slave Crimes," as if it is possible for a slave to commit a crime against a slavemaster.) The ones who felled the trees and cultivated the land and nursed white babies and helped rear them and laid railroad tracks and built levees and carried out a thousand additional tasks—these were the ones who suffered the additional abuse of being called "lazy." In short, the Black victims of lawlessness and lust and unspeakable acts of inhumanity become, in the American mind, the purveyors. There is a sense in which this phenomenon is repeated in other circumstances of extreme oppres-

TO BE SOLD & LET

BY PUBLIC AUCTION,

On MONDAY the 18th of MAY, 1829,

UNDER THE TREES.

FOR SALE,

THE THREE FOLLOWING

SLAVES,

VIZ.

HANNIBAL, about 30 Years old, an excellent House Servant, of Good Character.

WILLIAM, about 35 Years old, a Labourer.

NANCY, an excellent House Servant and Nurse.

The MEN belonging to "LEECH'S" Estate, and the WOMAN to Mrs. D. SMIT.

TO BE LET,

On the usual conditions of the Hirer finding them in Food, Clothing, and Medical Attendance.

THE FOLLOWING

MALE and FEMALE

SLAVES,

OF GOOD CHARACTERS.

ROBERT BAGLEY, about 20 Years old, a good House Servant.

WILLIAM BAGLEY, about 10 Years old a Labourer.

JOHN ARMS, about 16 Years old.

JACK ANTONIA, about 40 Years old, a Labourer.

PHILIP, an Excellent Fisherman.

HARRY, about 27 Years old, a good House Servant.

LUCY, a Young Woman of good Character, used to House Work and the Nursery.

ELIZA, an Excellent Washerwoman.

CLARA, an Excellent Washerwoman.

FANNY, about 14 Years old, House Servant.

SARAH, about 14 Years old, House Servant.

Also for Sale, at Eleven o'Clock,

Fine Rice, Gram, Paddy, Books, Muslins, Needles, Pins, Ribbons, &c. &c.

AT ONE O'CLOCK, THAT CELEBRATED ENGLISH HORSE,

BLUCHER.

Some dealers rented slaves on a contractual basis.
(*The Bettmann Archive*)

Slave policies became a profitable business for insurance companies. *(Negro History Associates)*

No. 2276

SLAVE POLICY.

𝔄merican 𝔏ife 𝔍nsurance

AND TRUST COMPANY,

Office, Walnut Street, S. E. Corner of Fourth.

PHILADELPHIA.

(CHARTER PERPETUAL,)

Insurance on the Life of

George

Slave of

Joseph Myers

AMOUNT $ *1000* INSURED.

Date of Policy *April 3rd 1858*

Term *Five Years*

Premium . . . . . . $ *17.40*
Policy fee, ... *2. —*

$ *19.40*

sion. In America, however, racism served to sharpen the edges of such attacks, to accentuate still further the inhumanity which lies at the core of the process.

Clearly, historians have devoted too little attention to the corrosive effects of slavery on White institutional and personality development. We are quite familiar with the work which has been done on how slavery damaged Black people. The implication has been that slavery did not grievously harm White institutions or White personality development. Sadly, White people seem to feel that, despite the severity of racism in the country, they have no serious personality problems which are directly related to racism.

Of course, Black folk, having lived through two and a half centuries of slavery and more than a hundred years of racism, discrimination, and segregation, are adult enough to realize that they have certain hang-ups. They realize that the American experiment has been a profoundly tragic one, while the overwhelming number of White people during and since slavery (including most historians) show not the slightest sign of recognizing the tragedy of American life, save possibly the Civil War experience, and then because so many White people were killing each other. Because White abolitionists recognized the tragedy and obscenity of slavery, they were viewed as fanatics and sometimes as lunatics. Considering the quarters from which they came, such attacks on Abolitionists should not surprise.

Certain historians tell us that the Afro-American, in the process of surviving in this land, indulged in certain infantile behavioral patterns which were, over a period of time, committed to psychological and spiritual marriage. Indeed, it has been suggested that Black people, owing to the severity of their ordeal and the awesome power of the slave master, began to identify with the aggressive overlord while giving survival primacy over all other considerations. If there is some kernel of truth in the Sambo thesis, then *there is abundant* evidence pointing to the possibility, given the intensity and pervasiveness of the oppression of Black people in American society, that White people, with *few exceptions, internalized the cultural virus of racism,* transmitted it through institutions, public and private, from decade to decade, from generation to generation down three and a half centuries to the present harsh reality.

It must have been racism in combination with, and perhaps indistinguishable from, the greed of slaveholders and those profiting from slavery which made possible the domestic slave trade, the movement of large numbers of slaves from areas in which they were no longer in great demand to areas of the Southwest to tame and cultivate the land and increase the political power of the slaveholding states. Washington, D.C., the nation's capitol, became the radiating center of this sordid practice, together with areas such as Alexandria, Baltimore, Richmond, and Annapolis. Banks, jails, and mortgage companies pro-

108

vided services for this "trade" in human beings, operating openly, as did, of course, the slave traders themselves.

As dehumanizing as the domestic slave trade was, even more despicable was slave breeding which was practiced (despite the disclaimers of certain historians such as Avery Craven) in the Upper South. This was the breeding of Black men and women for the purpose of producing more slaves to sell in areas further south and west. This institution, which flourished in Virginia and other Upper South areas, was one of the most diabolical that man has ever developed. Those who doubt that slave breeding was practiced by Southerners would do well to read the words of Du Bois on the moral degradation to which some southern Whites were driven by the institution of slavery:

> Southerners who had suckled food from black breasts vied with each other in fornication with black women, and even in beastly incest. They took the name of their fathers in vain to seduce their own sisters. Nothing—nothing that black folk did or said or thought or sang was sacred.

By 1860, as historian Kenneth Stampp has pointed out, hundreds of thousands of slaves, out of a population of only four million, were mulattoes. Only a relatively small number of Black people were without some White blood—this despite the talk of southerners about the desire to maintain the "purity" of the White race. The interest of White men in Black women was so great that White women by the millions during and following slavery were caused extreme embarrassment. Lillian Smith has brilliantly explored this aspect of Black-White relations.

By 1860 the slave states had a total population of almost thirteen million, of whom 8,898,000 were White, 3,954,000 slaves, and 280,-000 free Blacks. Contrary to the *Gone With The Wind* fantasy of very large numbers of well-to-do slaveowners with plantations populated with slaves extending as far as the eye could see, there were only about 2,000 slaveowners with one hundred or more slaves. Those with five or fewer slaves usually worked with them in the fields. The typical southerner was a nonslaveholder, though the typical southerner, sadly enough, identified with the slaveholding class, and that was his tragedy. This identification offered many poor Whites immense psychological satisfaction, which was as important to some as material wealth.

Behind the mythology of southern gentlemen and southern belles were, in the overwhelming majority of cases, the coarse people and coarse culture that one might suspect existed in a society so dependent on force for its viability. Indeed, save for the creativity of the slaves, the leisure which slavery afforded certain overlords and their

followers was not sufficient to arc the gap between hope and fulfill-
ment. White artistic and literary achievements during slavery were
profoundly inept and uninspired. The music of the slaves, as Du Bois
said, "was slavery's one redemption, distilled from the dross of its
dung."

Slavery debased Blacks but debased slaveholders, White people
generally, and America still more, cheapening and making relatively
unimportant in the eyes of most Whites the very lives of people of
color, male and female, old and young. Slavery laid foundations for
the present terror and lawlessness practiced against Black people in
this country and against people of color in other parts of the world.
Slavery paved the way for the indifference of White Americans toward the quality of their own lives.

We should bear in mind that Frederick Douglass, Henry Highland
Garnet, David Walker—indeed, practically all of the black Abolitionists—were aware of the detrimental impact of slavery on *all* Americans. Booker T. Washington, who could not be accused of being a
severe critic of White people, pointed out in *Up From Slavery* that
slavery had been harmful to master and slave, having pulled White
people down into the gutter. Black people, then, did not need instruc-
tion from Thomas Jefferson on the deep scars that slavery left on
the overlords. Yet today's historians might profit from Jefferson's remarks concerning how slavery had brutalized the master (whatever
the gains experienced by Whites through oppressing Blacks), for the
slaveowner was not only a participant in the barbarous practice; he
was, as Jefferson pointed out, the instigator.

It was this kind of attitude that helped to plant the
seeds of racism.　　　(*New York Historical Society*)

Exercises

1. The concept of freedom, which developed in the Renaissance, became "the freedom to destroy freedom." Discuss this quotation and give examples which illustrate it. Define the scope of the word "freedom" (that is, is its application limited or unlimited? In reference to what or whom? What implications does this have for the term "humanity," which is itself another concept which Renaissance Europe grappled with and sought to redefine?)

2. In what ways can the institution of slavery satisfy the lusts for power? What is meant here by power? (Are there different forms of power? Do they all derive ultimately from the same source? From different sources?)

3. Mr. Stuckey states that one finds racism at the base of American institutions from the time of their inception. How would you define this word? Professor Lynd, in another lesson, has spoken of prejudice and given a quotation from Thomas Jefferson to illustrate it? Can you perhaps find a common link between the two terms "assumptions" and "prejudice"?

4. In what way might the existence of racist assumptions on the part of one human community impede human growth within that community?

5. What is meant by the domestic slave trade?

6. Why do you suppose the question of slave breeding (whether it existed or not, and, if so, to what degree) is such a controversial one? Is the essential issue one of historical accuracy? Or is it something else?

7. Summarize in one sentence the main point that Mr. Stuckey makes in this lesson. (Such a summary sentence occurs in the lesson itself. Where would it be likely to occur? Can you locate it?)

1. Mr. Stuckey points to the dual role in which the White man saw himself in relation to the Black: that of enslaver and Christianizer. Take as the topic for a hypothetical research paper "The Role of the Missionary in the Context of American Institutionalized Slavery." You will want to know such things as what groups of people carried on missionary work (ministers, devout laymen, abolitionists, slaveholders?) Was missionary work organized as it later was in Africa? Did missionary work among the slaves differ markedly from missionary work among the Indians? Did missionary work precede or follow enslavement? Were passages from Scripture chosen which tended to accommodate themselves to the institution, that is, which stressed Christian humility and submission to higher authority?

111

2. Mr. Stuckey suggests that historians in the past, and in the present, have devoted all too little attention to the corrosive effects of slavery upon White institutional and personality development. How many passages have you come across, in your readings, which, in effect, deal with this aspect? Read a few stories by writers of what is sometimes called the Southern Renaissance. These are not historians but fiction writers, and their treatment of the problem is likely to be indirect. Choose from among William Faulkner, Katherine Anne Porter, Robert Penn Warren, Eudora Welty, and Tennessee Williams.

3. Do some research on the underground slave trade conducted after 1808. From where did the additional slaves come? Who were the slave traders? What were the methods used to smuggle them into the country? Did the government adopt a lax or stiff attitude toward enforcing the law?

4. Do some research on the domestic slave trade. How were the slaves located, traded, and transported? Was trade carried on with all age groups? Were all such ventures profitable to the trader? Was the trader an entrepreneur, or was this merely a part-time venture for him? Compare your findings with what you have learned about the underground slave trade.

Suggested Readings

A Documentary History of the Negro in the United States, vol. I. By Herbert Aptheker. Citadel, New York, 1951, reissued 1969. A standard work, very useful on many levels.

The Abolitionists. By Richard O. Curry. Holt, Rinehart and Winston, New York, 1965.

To Be A Slave. By Julius Lester. Dial, New York, 1968. A book about the condition of slavery told by slaves.

The Burden of Southern History. By C. Vann Woodward. Louisiana State University Press, Baton Rouge. A book about Southern history and the making of the Southern attitude.

Black Expression. By Addison Gayle, Jr. Weybright and Tally, New York, 1969. See one, "On Folk Culture." pp. 3–47.

SLAVERY AND THE
BUILDING OF AMERICA

Sterling Stuckey

Whatever the achievements of Blacks in this country, they were made at grave costs. Thousands, hundreds of thousands, perhaps millions of Black people were broken by the experience of slavery over two and a half centuries. But somehow Black people managed, despite the brutality of slavery, to fashion a subterranean world and to create a certain life style, a certain system of values, a certain angle of vision, and a view of the world that was not shaped by the oppressor.

W. E. B. Du Bois wrote that the gifts of song and brawn were among the greatest contributions of Black people to America.

First, let us consider the gift of brawn, the gift of muscle that enabled the country to be built much faster than it would have been otherwise. Blacks worked as bondsmen, and, in an overwhelming majority of cases, without ever receiving pay for their labor. They worked the principal crops in this country: cotton, tobacco, indigo, sugar cane, and rice. They endured great hardships; many perished in the process.

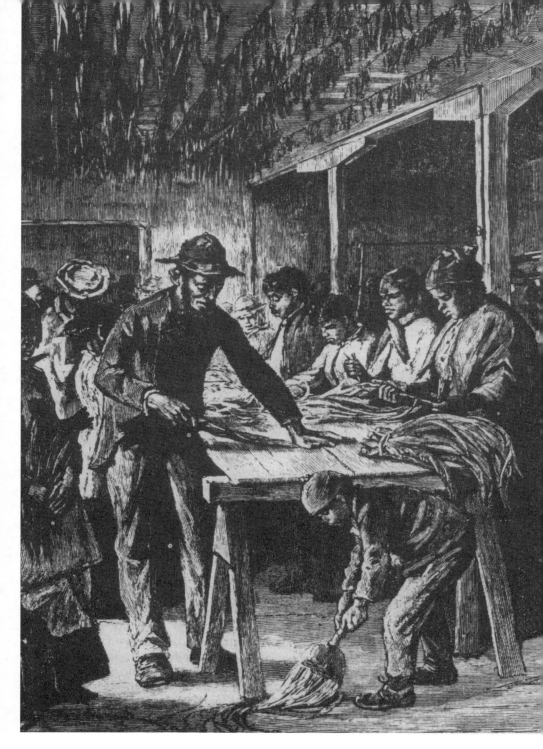

(*Virginia State Library*)

The story is yet to be told in its entirety; but slaves played a tremendous role in laying railroad, in building levees in the South, in clearing and cultivating land in the South and Southwest. They did the dirty work for White people. They washed their dirty clothes, as Jimmy Baldwin has said, and served them their brandy and therefore were in a pretty good position to know how clean they were. They cooked the food and scrubbed the floors. They provided the overlords with ease, with comfort, with money.

They worked in factories, in foundries, and sometimes in mines. They provided the overwhelming majority of skilled labor, in the Southern countryside as well as in the cities—roughly four-fifths of the skilled labor. Having given the country some two and a half centuries of unrequited toil, the Blacks played a significant role indeed in building the country—a role not even approximated by any other minority, a role very disproportionate to their numbers. Bishop Turner had this labor and suffering in mind when he said that Blacks had a thousand times more right to this country than any other people.

Another gift that Blacks gave to the country, as Du Bois has pointed out, was the gift of song, a gift that has been misunderstood, scorned, and even caricatured. Historians such as U. B. Phillips completely misinterpreted the meaning of Afro-American song during slavery. Even today, historians have not properly assessed the importance of slave folklore to slave life and to American culture.

Slave folklore, as reflected in slave song, is an important indicator of how slaves actually felt about their condition. Du Bois once said, in *The Souls of Black Folk*, that song was the slaves' "one articulate message to the world." Slave lore enables us to get inside the slave to discover how he felt about his condition.

Frederick Douglass, who was a slave and should have known, said that upon coming to the North he was astonished to find people who spoke of the singing among slaves as evidence of their contentment and happiness. Decades later the young Du Bois, among the first knowledgeable critics of the spiritual, said that he found White Americans as late as 1903 still telling Black Americans that "life was joyous and happy, the Black slave, careless and happy."

Du Bois' response, in *The Souls of Black Folks*, in the chapter "Of Our Spiritual Strivings," wrote: "I can easily believe this of some, of many." But, he continued, the songs "are the music of an unhappy people, of the children of disappointment. They tell of death and suffering and unvoiced longing toward a truer world, of misty wanderings and hidden ways."

Frederick Douglass, probably referring to the spirituals, said that the songs of slaves represented the sorrows of the slave's heart, serving to relieve the slave only as an aching heart is relieved by its tears. "I have often sung," he wrote, "to drown my sorrow, but seldom to express my happiness. Crying for joy and singing for joy were alike uncommon to me while in the jaws of slavery."

Sterling Brown has much to tell us about the poetry and the meaning of these songs; he observed, "As the best expression of the slave's deepest thoughts and yearnings, the spiritual speaks with convincing finality against the legend of contented slavery." Brown states that though the creators of the spirituals, those poor, illiterate Black slave geniuses, "looked toward heaven and found their triumph there, they did not blink their eyes to the trouble here." The spirituals, according to Brown, "never tell of joy in the good old days" of slavery; "the only joy in the spirituals is in dreams of escape." In Brown's opinion, these songs "tell of this life, of rollin' through an unfriendly world." And he cites these lines from the spirituals to prove his point:

Oh by and by, by and by,
I'm going to lay down this heavy load;
My way is cloudy;
Oh, stand in the storm, it won't be long,
We'll anchor by and by.
Lord, help me from sinking down; and
Don't know what my mother wants to stay here for,
This old world ain't been no friend to her.

Are we to believe, asks Brown, that the slave singing,

I been rebuked, I been scorned,
Done had a hard time shows you're born

referred to his being outside any true religion? A reading of additional spirituals indicates that they did not represent what White people regarded as the true religion? Whites were not given to intimacy with God, or Jesus, as were the Black Slaves. One slave wrote:

When I get to heaven,
Going to be at ease,
Me and my God going to do as we please.
Gonna chatter with the Father,
Argue with the Son
Tell um about the world
I just come from.

Other lines from slave lore:

Talk about me much as you please,
Talk about me much as you please,
Chil'en, talk about me much as you please,
Going to talk about you when I get on my knees.

And they weren't talking about children, they were talking about White people. . . .

Many skilled slaves were able to hire themselves for work at a minimal wage. Here are coopers at work. (*Prints Division, New York Public Library*)

By the mid 1600s, the European market was flooded with tobacco and prices fell; thus, colonial planters turned their attention to the cultivation of rice, sugar cane, indigo, lumber, and other crops.   (*Prints Division, New York Public Library*)

The spiritual "Samson," as Vincent Harding has pointed out, probably contained more for some slaves than mere Biblical implications:

> He said, "And if I had it my way,"
> He said, "And if I had it my way,"
> He said, "And if I had my way, I'd tear the building down."
> He said, "And now I got my way,
> And now I got my way,
> And now I got my way,
> And I'll tear this building down."

Some who sang these lines, Harding suggests, might well have meant tearing down the structure of slavery itself. If so, it was the slavery equivalent of today's "Burn, Baby, Burn."

At times, slaves created great poetry as well as great music. One genius among the slaves couched his and their desire for freedom in a magnificent line of verse:

> After God's powerful voice had rung through heaven and down in hell,
> My dungeon shook and my chains fell,
> My dungeon shook and my chains fell.

Frederick Douglass informs us that slaves also sang ironic seculars about the institution of slavery. He reports having heard them sing:

> We raise the wheat,
> They give us the corn
> We sift the meal,
> They give us the husk,
> We peel the meat,
> They give us the skin,
> And that's the way they take us in.

Slaves would often stand back and see the tragicomic aspects of their situations; slavery was an absurdity, and slaves were capable of seeing it. Racism in America today is also an absurdity, and some blacks still have the capacity to laugh at that absurdity. But what Whites have not recognized is that, as Sterling Brown says, the laughter was laughter out of hell—not any mere Sambo posturing, or Sambo laughter, but laughter out of hell, as in this song:

> Run, nigger, run,
> The patrolers will catch you,
> Run, nigger, run,
> It's almost day,
> That nigger run,

119

That nigger flew,
That nigger tore his shirt in two.

And he's not putting down "niggers." From the slave's point of view, that was a beautiful, beautiful nigger doing that running. (He was getting away.)

That could not be taught by White people. Only a Black could teach this particular kind of song. Because blacks use *nigger* in a variety of ways.

And there are these lines:

My old missus promised me, when she died,
She'd set me free.
She lived so long that her head got bald,
And she give up the notion of dying at all.

And slave work songs such as,

Long summer day make a white man lazy,
Long summer day.
Long summer day makes a nigger run away far,
Long summer day.

Other slaves sang lines indicating their distaste for slavery. They were not insensitive to what was going on.

Ol' massa and ol' missy sittin' in the parlor,
Just a figurin' and a-plannin' how to work a nigger harder.

And there are these bitter lines:

Missus in the big house, mammy in the yard,
Missus holding her white hand, mammy workin' hard,
    mammy workin' hard, mammy workin' hard.
Missus holding her white hand, mammy workin' hard.
Old Marse riding all the time, niggers working 'round,
Marse sleeping day time, niggers digging in the ground,
    niggers digging in the ground, niggers digging in the ground.
Marse sleeping day time, niggers digging in the ground.

And,

When I was young and in my prime,
Sunk my axe deep every time

A particular aspect of Black lore suggests that the average slave probably felt that White men individually were weak, that they were strong only in groups. As Sterling Brown said: "They don't come by ones, they don't come by twos, but they come by tens."

120

From the "John Henry" work song, spiritual descendant of Trickster John of slave folklore we hear:

> A man ain't nothing but a man,
> But before I'll let that steam driver beat me down,
> I'll die with my hammer in my hand.

Other Blacks, a little less willing to die, and a bit more skeptical about beating steam drivers down, have written and sung,

> This old hammer, huh,
> Gleam like silver, huh,
> Shine like gold, baby,
> Shine like gold.
> This old hammer killed John Henry,
> Twon't kill me, baby,
> Twon't kill me.

And there were slaves singing lines that suggested African consciousness, as in the meeting of Vesey and others in Charleston. They sang these lines, not a spiritual but a hymn. The song was probably written by Vesey himself.

> Hail! all Hail! ye Afric' clan,
> Hail! ye oppressed, ye Afric' band,
> Who toil and sweat in slavery bound
> And when your health and strength are gone
> Are left to hunger and to mourn,
> Let independence be your aim,
> Ever mindful what is work.
> Pledge your bodies for the prize,
> Pile them even to the skies!

For anyone who suggests that the Vesey conspiracy was nothing more than loose talk from the lips of a few aggrieved and bitter men, let him consider those lines:

> Pledge your bodies for the prize,
> Pile them even to the skies.

Blacks sang of Nat Turner, of the meaning of Nat Turner to them:

> You might be rich as cream,
> And ride your coach with a four horse team,
> But you can't keep the world from moving around,
> Nor Nat Turner from gaining ground.
> And your name that might be Caesar sure,
> And got you a cannon that can shoot a mile or more,

121

But you can't keep the world from moving around,
Nor Nat Turner from gaining ground.

A great many slaves, when the Civil War began, realized for the first time in their lives that they could make a decision that might guarantee their emancipation. Of course, during the earlier period, how was one to know whether one would be successful in a slave revolt? So, until then, the great majority of slaves resisted slavery in the only ways they could, ways which usually fell short of liberation.

But when emancipation seemed possible, as Du Bois described, in a brilliant recreation of that period in *Black Reconstruction*, thousands of slaves took decisive action.

> There came the slow looming of emancipation. Crowds and armies of the unknown, inscrutable . . . Yankees, cruelty behind and before, rumors of a new slave trade, but slowly, continuously, the wild truth, the bitter truth, the magic truth came surging through. There was to be a new freedom, and a black nation went tramping after the armies, no matter what it suffered, no matter how it was treated, no matter how it died.

Thousands tramped after the Sherman forces on his march to the sea. Du Bois brought together the insights of the poet as well as historian in getting inside the slaves at the moment of emancipation:

> There was joy in the South; it rose like perfume, like a prayer. Men stood quivering, slim dark girls, wild and beautiful, with wrinkled hair, wept silently. Young women, black, tawny, white and golden, lifted shivering hands, and old and broken mothers, black and grey, raised great voices and shouted to God across the fields and up to the rocks and the mountains. Some sang:

> Slavery chain done broke at last, broke at last, broke at last,
> Slavery chain done broke at last, going to praise God till I die.
> I did tell him how I suffer in the dungeon and the chain,
> And the days I went with head bowed down,
> And my broken flesh and pain.
> Slavery chain done broke at last, broke at last, broke at last,
> Slavery chain done broke at last,
> Going to praise God till I die.

Some historians have suggested that it was the shock of the Civil War, like so many other shocks, that caused the slaves to be concerned about emancipation. But a close reading of slave work-songs and slave spirituals does not suggest this. Four years before the outbreak of the war some sang:

> Come all my brethren, let us take a rest,
> While the moon shines bright and clear,

The economy of the new colony was built upon the deliberate and systematic enslavement (with all the barbarities it entailed) of black people.   (*Culver Pictures, Inc.*)

Old master died and left us all at last,
And has gone at the bar to appear,
Old master is dead and lying in his grave,
And our blood will now cease to flow.
He will no more trample on the neck of the slave,
He's gone where the slaveholders go.
Hand up the shovel and the hoe,
I don't care whether I work or no,
Old master's gone to the slaveholder's rest,
He's gone where they all ought to go.

How can one call people who produce that kind of poetry, that kind of music, Sambos? How can one say that they were insensitive to their status, that they did not contemplate their low condition?

This music can be viewed for what it tells us explicitly from an examination of the words, or it can be viewed as music itself, for elevating and poignant sounds at the heart of the spirituals or the power and drive and vivid imagery of the work song.

Though time does not permit an exploration of folk tales, it should be remarked that Afro-American folk tales often speak of the weak animal outwitting the strong animal—the slave outwitting the master. The symbolism suggests that a great many slaves were well aware of their condition; they had not accepted the master's vision of them as slaves; and they were going about the job of defining themselves—at least on the level of art.

There can be no more eloquent testimony of the meaning and significance of slave songs than the fact that in the Freedom Movement over the past decade or so—the Blacks who sat in at lunch counters, the Blacks who were involved in Freedom Rides, the Blacks who were involved in voter registration in the South—all sang slave songs.

Michael rowed a boat ashore,
Just like a tree standing by the water,
We shall not be moved.

Du Bois put it well: "We have given the country our gifts of song, brawn and spirit. We have provided a simple oasis of faith in a dusty desert of dollars and smartness."

And historians would do well to listen to Du Bois, who was the first and only historian of recent generations to deal perceptively and sensitively with slave folklore. Du Bois was perfectly correct when he said that the songs of slaves represented slavery's "one redemption, distilled from the dross of its dung."

124

Exercises

1. Name two or three major occupations—aside from plantation farming—in which Black slave labor was a major factor.

2. What was the medium by which the slaves' "view of the world . . . not shaped by the oppressor" was expressed? Can you state in any detail the techniques the slave used to communicate his view of the world within this medium?

3. Mr. Stuckey is especially adept at drawing parallels between the reality of slavery and the reality of present-day America. Can you find any instances of it in this lesson? What is the effect of such parallels?

4. What does Sterling Brown mean by the term "laughter out of hell"? What associations are evoked by the term "hell"? What is the tonal quality of this laughter?

5. Which gifts does Dr. Du Bois state the Black slave gave to America?

6. "They washed their dirty clothes, as Jimmy Baldwin has said, and served them their brandy and therefore were in a good position to know how clean they were." How many levels of meaning does the word "clean" carry? Why would a slave be in a good position to know this? The reference to James Baldwin serves to emphasize yet a different aspect: Does each party—master and slave—view each other in the same light? Which one understands the other more intimately? Why?

7. The cry of back wages due for unpaid slave labor is a manifestation of awareness among Blacks of our contribution to the building of America. Can you point to any examples of this demand, in any form, among Blacks? (Do not limit yourself to the most militant groups.)

8. With reference to the song "Run, Nigger, Run," why does Mr. Stuckey say it is the kind of song only a Black could teach? Recall his earlier statements regarding a subterranean world with its distinctive life-styles. Suppose a White teacher had knowledge of this world (as he could conceivably have at the present day due to all the published research). Would he then also be able to teach the song? Why or why not?

9. What kinds of knowledge can be gained from the study of slave lore?

10. What is Mr. Stuckey's major theme in this lesson, which he illustrates by selections from the spirituals?

1. Two interpretations of the meaning of the spirituals are 1) that they represent the slaves' peculiar interpretation of Christianity and his eager expectation in the hereafter of those joys denied him in life on earth; and 2) that they represent a hidden spirit of revolt against his circumstances in this life and often relay messages of planned escape. Compare these two with a third, advanced by Jahnheinz Jahn, which sees the metaphysical beliefs of the slaves in the Spirituals as part of an unbroken tradition brought from Africa. The Spirituals therefore reflect the African life-style and world-view. (See Jahnheinz Jahn, *Neo-African Literature, A History of Black Writing.* Grove Press, New York, 1968.) Which of these three schools of thought casts the slave in the most authentically human frame (that is, reflects the profundity and diversity of human experience and feeling)? Which *seems* the most convincing, based on its presentation and documentation? Which do you think comes (or come) closest to the reality of slave life?

2. Just as in the case of the spiritual, there has been much controversy surrounding the animal figures of Black folklore: whether they are of African importation and/or African-American invention; whether they are adaptations of the White folklore with which the slaves came into contact or whether the line of descent is more complicated still. A brief statement of the problem is to be found in Sterling Brown's essay, "Negro Folk Expression" (in *Black Expression*, ed. Addison Gayle, Jr.). Write out, on the basis of your readings in folklore, brief character sketches of the following animals:
   a) the rabbit (Brer Rabbit)
   b) the spider (Anasi)
   c) the terrapin
   d) the fox (Brer Fox)
   e) the wolf (Brer Wolf)

3. Write out character sketches of the following animals, which appear in African tales:
   a) Leo the lion
   b) Reynard the fox
   c) the crow
   d) Isengrin the wolf

4. The students who have worked on one of the groups of tales could come together in a panel discussion to present their summaries and to discuss differences and similarities. What are the similarities among the stories? What were the people like who created or perpetuated the stories (that is, American and West Indian Blacks; precolonial Africans; medieval Europeans). In particular, what was their social status in relation to other members of their societies?

126

5. Compile a bibliography of literature written on the spiritual. Make two lists; one, of those works which see the spiritual as a reworking, by Africans, of the Christian concept of God and salvation, and the other, of those which see the spirituals as symbolic songs of rebellion and revolt and of involvement in the life on earth. It is not necessary to read the entire book or article; usually a scanning of one or two pages of the introduction or conclusion, or reading comments in book reviews and annotated bibliographies will suffice to indicate the author's school of thought. Note in particular the race of the author (if available) and the date of publication. Can you establish a correlation between the period when written and school of thought?

Suggested Readings

The Political Economy of Slavery. By Eugene D. Genovese. Pantheon, New York, 1964.

The Negro in the Making of America. By Benjamin Quarles. Collier, New York, 1964. A concise overview of Afro-American History.

Neglected History. By Charles H. Wesley. Essays in Negro-American History, Central State College Press, Wilberforce, Ohio, 1965. See chapter two, "Politics and Abolition."

Four Took Freedom. By Philip Sterling and Rayford Logan. Zenith Books, Doubleday, New York, 1967. Lives of Harriet Tubman, Frederick Douglass, Robert Smalls, and Blanche K. Bruce.

Pioneers and Patriots. By Livinia Dobler and Edgar A. Toppin. Zenith Books, Doubleday, New York, 1965. The lives of six Black leaders of the Revolutionary Era.

127

PART III: CONCLUSION:

by John Henrik Clarke

THE RESHAPING OF THE AFRICAN MIND DURING THE AFTERMATH OF SLAVERY

John Henrik Clarke

I had an encounter on Friday, March 29, 1996, in relationship to the debate over Professor Lefkowitz's book, *Not Out of Africa*, that left me in good fighting shape. I will speak about it briefly, then go on to our subject, because the subject of last night's discussion relates to the subject of today: the enslavement of the African mind. I was delighted, but not by what was said on the platform so much, because I had to discuss with three white people who seemed to have the assumption that African people are not thinkers, and were using this assumption as the basis of their intent to re-enslave our minds so that they can re-enslave Africa. The female panelist, Mary Lefkowitz, uses her book, *Not Out of Africa,* as a rationale to say that nothing we have ever said about our own history is valid. By her own admission, she discovered African history maybe four years ago and she is criticizing J.A. Rogers who devoted over fifty years of his life to the discovery of the African personality in world history. She is critical of all of our senior historians, none of whom she has read with any thoroughness or respect, including many she did not know at all.

People think that their whiteness in itself makes them an authority on everything Black. They think that they can proclaim something to be so without knowing what they are proclaiming. The other panelists, Professor Martin Bernal, a paternalistic, white sympathizer for black causes has made a quick reputation writing about people he has recently discovered.   His two volume work, *Black Athena*, basically is interesting, but contains not one new bit of evidence that we did not already have.   I am not so much as angry with Martin Bernal as I am angry with all of the blacks who hail him, reward him and pat him on the back. They assume that he is a kind of new messiah,   but he has rewritten,   and poorly at that, what competent Blacks and whites had been saying before he was born.   Many of these writers we haven't paid enough attention to.   Black colleges have invited Professor Bernal to give him awards and little taps on his shoulder,   and   they haven't read any of Dr. ben-Jochannan's books on the same subject,   books which are more informative. Bernal took information directly from Dr. ben-Jochannan's works, with very few footnotes or credits given.

Dr. Ben is a personal friend and colleague and we have personal fights among ourselves, but they stay strictly between Dr. Ben and me.   Most of our fights are over methodology;   scholars argue over methodology   when   they discuss   approaches to things.   That doesn't mean I want anyone to take sides in these fights because these fights are between the two of us.   We can work them out;   we don't need any referee.   I just don't think Dr. Ben has done the best by Dr. Ben.   If I try to scold him it's not because I differ with him.   I argue with him because he hasn't done the best by himself. He's got so much information in his head he should never waste his   time telling those silly sex stories.   What I'm saying is that I defend him against people like Lefkowitz,   because Lefkowitz doesn't even know enough to stand in judgment on the monumental work he has already contributed;   she only discovered him the day before yesterday.   And that was my criticism of her.

Martin Bernal's work is of no great revelation. He has made some concessions to African people, but the concessions he has made to us and our con- tribution to history is minor in comparison to the concession that Gerald Massey made one hundred years ago, and minor in comparison to the work that Albert Churchward has made in his *Signs and Symbols of Primordial Man* and *Origin of Religion*. We need to understand that Professor Bernal is not a pioneer in exposing the fact that European history in relationship to African history is a fraud and a fakery. However, the trap he fell into in this discussion was his emphasis on anti-Semitism in literature. When I challenged him to tell me what a Semite is, and made several other points, he hemmed and hawed and tried to explain it.

He finally had to make the concession that it was a linguistic word and not an ethnic word. The other panelist, Professor Rogers, has edited a book with Professor Lefkowitz attacking Bernal's book, *Black Athena*; it's called *Black Athena Revisited*.

What almost single-handedly carried the day and held that discussion together was Utrice Leid, who was master of ceremonies. We've got to give this woman some more recognition for her many talents. She was right on top of the situation and she would not let them get away with anything; she knew how to question them. This is what we have to start understanding: we can question these people; they're on shaky grounds and they're afraid. Professor Lefkowitz was literally trembling because she was in an area over her head intellectually. We haven't confronted these people, the columnist George Wells and people like that; they need to be confronted.

The most stimulating thing about the evening was the audience — not one unintelligent question. In fact, we didn't have enough time to answer all the questions. There was a Brother who used to come to my lectures occasionally; he came with references in his pockets, in his stockings, all over. When he took the floor he started quoting the Catholic church's opinion on the subject. Then he said, "If I'm wrong, your scholarly references are wrong. Not only are they wrong according to today's scholars, they are wrong according to past scholars, ... not our's, yours."

No one knows how to challenge people on this

basis. So far as I'm concerned, it was one of the most successful encounters of a Black audience with whites who are allegedly supposed to be authorities on Blacks. I was rejuvenated because I think we've waited too long to do this. The First World Lectures, those long lectures delivered here and there, are finally beginning to pay off; some of us are finally learning how to confront our white enemies in relationship to their misinformation on our history. This is all this long fight has been about. I could have done a whole lot of things other than devote my life to this subject. But last night I saw it pay off. It wasn't about money in the first place because I could have had money doing something else. It wasn't so much about applause or pats on the back, or bad banquet dinners which I've eaten too much of. It was about seeing my people take charge and defend themselves based on information they understand about themselves and not flinching or retreating but standing straight before their enemy and giving no ground at all.

I had to make it plain from the beginning when they listed our discussion as a debate that on this subject, to which I have devoted all of my adult life, I will not debate. I will discuss the subject; I will only debate with my equals. All others I teach. So if you are ready to put your mind in the posture of the student, the professor is ready to teach. Now for the subject of this evening.

The subject of this evening is the Aftermath of Slavery: the Making of the African Mind during that Aftermath in the Midst of Emancipation. The subject is a contradiction in terms because I maintain that there is no aftermath of slavery because only the slave can free the slave. Until the slave frees the slave, the aftermath of slavery is another form of slavery. What I am going to be talking about are the different forms of slavery that followed the assumption of Emancipation and the shaping of the African mind in the African world that programmed African people into another form of slavery today more dangerous than the original slavery ever was. As a result, we are further from liberation, right now, than we were ten years before Emancipation and one hundred years after Emancipation. This is because our enemies are geniuses at chicanery and we are unsuspecting in relationship to our enemy. Because we get a few tokens, a few smiles here and there, we engage in wars among ourselves which are nothing but comparative studies of slavery. My slave master is better than your slave master, we say. My slave master had a ceremony called Crop Over in which the governor danced with the best looking Black girls on the island. My slave master sent some of his children which he sired by raping my women, he sent some of them to school for an education. That's a comparative study of the debauchery of slavery and a few tokens in relationship to slavery, but that is not Emancipation.

So immediately after the phony ceremony of Emancipation, they began to prepare the African mind for the new slavery. And immediately after the African independence explosion, they began to prepare the African mind, and the mind of the world to accept the recolonization of Africa. The vehicle for the recolonization was to impose upon Africa the concept of a state alien to Africa. The African has never lived in a European-type concept of a nation-state; the nation-state is un-African; the African has always lived in a territorial state. The territorial state is a cultural state consisting of many different people, many different cultures; cultures fertilizing cultures; cultures stimulating cultures. There is intellectual growth by virtue of the free exchange of cultures — free exchange without animosity.

This is the kind of state the European has never produced and is morally incapable of producing. When he produces the multicultural state, one culture must be predominant over the other to the extent that most of the people in the state are reduced to vassalage. We have not taken into consideration the fact that during the height of the Roman and Greek empires the majority of the population, as much as 85%, were slaves, and while the European was creating a concept that he called democracy, most of the people preaching the concept went home and were served by slaves. So democracy was meant for a select few; it never was a mass movement for the greater number — neither in Rome, nor in Greece.

Another thing that has to be taken into consideration is that Rome and Greece were not European creations because at the time of Rome and Greece there was no politically functioning Europe. How can someone create something for someone else when they have not created a shoe for themselves or a house with a window? Rome and Greece were actually Mediterranean-inspired nations who took their impetus from North Africa and Western Asia and the islands of the Mediterranean, and there was not one organized state in Europe at the time.

The scattered tribes in Europe accepted the challenge of Rome and Greece and reacted to their fears. Once Rome and Greece began to prey on them, Europeans trying to imperialize other Europeans, they banded together to fight Rome and Greece. In getting together to fight Rome and Greece, they created the European state. If anybody has any information to the contrary, I want to hear it. So the concept of Europe bringing light to the world is a lie that we have accepted. It is part of the enslavement of our intellectual capacity that haunts us to this day: thinking two countries (Rome and Greece) brought light and civilization to the world when they did not get it from within themselves because they didn't even have it within themselves.

If you study Rome, you've got to study the Etruscans; they were the forerunners of Rome. The forerunners of Greece were an African and a Mediterranean people. The Mediterranean/North African/Western Asian world was the functioning world as they knew it. However, the incubator, the feeder of that world, was the great world to the south, the lower Nile Valley. The Nile was a great cultural highway stretching four thousand miles into the body of Africa. Down that four thousand mile valley came a mixture of people, the greatest mixture of skill, technology, intellectual know-

how, to create the nation that ultimately became
the nation that the Greeks called Egypt. Egypt
was, as Dr. Ben has told you a number of times,
the culmination of a number of African civilizations
coming together to create a single civilization that
came much later.

When the Sahara dried up, most of these technicians moved toward the Nile; some moved toward the
Niger; some moved down into what is now Nigeria.
If you read Henri Lhote's work on the Tassili
frescoes, we can see the swayback cow on the
walls in the Sahara drawings: that same cow is in
Nigeria right now. This is an area in which I have
done primary research.

When catastrophe hits the Africans in one place,
they move to another place. Once the invaders hit
North Africa, the Africans who had moved down and
built the civilization we now call Egypt did not
leave Africa; they moved down into the physical
body of Africa. So the descendants of the Ancient
Egyptians are still in Africa. If you can, go to
Senegal, go to Somalia, go to Ethiopia. Take the
pictures of the statues in Ancient Egypt; you can
find those facial features 100% duplicated down in
the South, the same people. Right now the great
tragedy in Africa is that many of these same people,
having been driven out of the Sudan by slave trading
Arabs, are standing at the border of their country
waiting to get back into a country that they
created. They were driven out by a heartless,
corrupt invader that people are now making rational-
izations for and trying to pretend that these people
are not in the slave trade. When they entered
Africa, they were in the slave trade and they never
got out of it. They were in the slave trade before
Islam, and they were in the slave trade after Islam.
We have to learn to identify exactly what is
slavery. Now let's begin.

Professor Kojo of the CUNY Graduate Center said
years ago in a conference at Queens College on
slavery that the condition of slavery is not the
condition of being poor. Many people are poor and
they are not slaves. The condition of slavery is
not the condition of working hard. Many people work

135

hard and they are not slaves. The condition of slavery is not being able to determine your own destiny. So today we have slaves with horn-rimmed glasses, attaché cases, split-level houses in the suburbs, Wall Street jobs and wives to pick them up at the train station, and they are still slaves.

In Europe up until the Protestant Reformation, they had a system of feudalism that was not tantamount to slavery; it was actual slavery. They had a system of slavery where some rich, feudal thugs could take over your land and you had nowhere else to go, so you had to work for them for a pittance or just for your keep. We are talking about whites exploiting whites; had you understood this system in history you would not be expecting anything from them. If they did this to their own people, what can you expect them to do to you? They don't know enough about your history to know the system of honor and morality that existed among you, and they imposed upon you a system with a lack of honor or morality which existed among them. Even if they knew what we had, they still would not have known how to respect it.

The main difference between European and African values is their attitude toward women. To the European a woman was seen as booty in war; and because she did not have to be asked for, she was seen as common property. She was common property due to the fact that her husband could sell her without her consent. Remember when Shakespeare died he left his wife his second best bed. He was kind. So if you look at how your enemy treated each other, how do you expect them to treat you?

During the Crusades, we are now into the 1000s A.D., the old Lords went on the Crusades searching for the Holy Grail that wasn't lost in the first place and wasn't holy in the second place. While they were on the Crusades the young lords made a concession: that is the right of first night. If you were a slave on my property and if you married, I had the right to sleep with your wife the first night. The young Lords gave up this privilege. After all, the Lord can sleep with her anytime he wants to because he can just command

136

it.   There is nothing she can do about it;   she's
living on his land.   Either get off the land or
submit.   So they let him have the first night;
maybe after that he would leave her alone.   The old
Lords weren't too happy about this major concession.
I am saying that this was a minor concession that
Europeans had made to the basic human rights of
Europeans,   a thing like giving the man a right to
be with his own wife the first night of their
marriage.   Where were you in the 1000s A.D.?

The empire of Ghana was flourishing.   It was
during this same period that you produced a great
King,   King Tenkamenin.   Before him,   there was
another king who took pride in being able to feed
masses of people.   Sometimes he would announce in
the morning,   "I'd like a few people to drop in for
lunch,   maybe 10,000."   When they got there the
food was ready.   The cows were killed,   the spit
was set up,   the meat was sliced and the tables were
set.   What does this tell you?   That the kitchen
was organized as well as the army,   and the army was
organized as the state.   I'm talking about human
organization in Africa at a time when Europeans were
vassal slaves.   You cannot make the comparative
statement;   you will have a hard time comparing
yourself with other people when you realize that at
times you were so far above them that there can be
no contest.   Up until now you have had a hard time
looking beyond your slavery mentality to a time
before someone introduced that mentality into
your mind.   What we have to deal with is before
and after.   The after is still with us,   and
the after is going to destroy us unless we make a
change and make it very soon.   We have to stop
depending on someone else's mind to tell us about
ourselves.   I note Tenkamenin,   his predecessor,
and other greats   because Europe had not worked its
way out of feudalism as yet.   They had just begun
the Crusades,   which were to last for a couple of
hundred years.

King Tenkamenin was known as the king who rode
out every day,   twice a day.   He would ride out

among the population and administer justice. It was a democratic monarchy; no one had to move from his presence until they were satisfied that justice had been done in their case. No one could be barred from approaching the King. He would ride out another time in the day, parading his royal dogs, and the horses were dressed better than the then kings of Europe; he would ride out in splendor to let people know he was still on the throne and the situation was still under control. To stabilize his horses, he used a large nugget of gold; the the horses' reins were looped through the lump of gold. Nobody was stealing gold; there was plenty of gold. We flaunted it; maybe that is why we lost it — too many other people knew about it.

We had this and Europe still hadn't produced a good house with a window. They were still partly coming out of the ice age. This is something I learned after I read Arthur Schomburg's essay, "The Negro Digs Up His Past." I discovered that I came from a people older than Europe, older than oppression, older than slavery. I started looking at the European and I said, "These people got here day before yesterday; I hope they can make it."

Now the passing of King Tenkamenin came at a time when Islam had invaded West Africa and moved down into the Western Sudan with the intent of Islamizing Africa or destroying it. I am saying that the intent of Islam in the eleventh century, the intent of Islam in the twentieth century, and the intent of Islam in the twenty-first century has not changed one iota. I'm saying that Quaddafi's intent to move to the South and to use the blacks in Chad and Niger against other non-Muslim Blacks has not changed one iota. They came into the country as slave traders and they still are slave traders. We have an illusion about the intent of the invader, but nobody has come into Africa to do African people any favors.

Ancient Ghana was destroyed by Moslem invasions. The Akan people, living in a kingdom of their own development, moved to the South and established themselves on the Volta River. They restructured their nation early in the eighteenth century to escape this slavery. Ultimately, the two nations to follow would become Islamic and the Royal family, the court and part of the military would save them. But the intent, not that a religion ever entered a continent without the intent of slavery, has not changed since the day of their entry. Christianity has not been much different; they differ only in methodology. So if you think there has been a period of emancipation, you misunderstand the sham of Emancipation and the myth of Emancipation and the manipulation of the African mind.

After the gradual destruction of these states and something which we had better study seriously, which we have ignored for too long, is the invasion of the Western Sudan in 1591. These were North African Moslems against the Moslems inland. It was a violation of the basic tenet that is supposed to govern their faith; it was Moslem against Moslem. No Moslem is supposed to lift arms against another Moslem. The Arabs have done this consistently, and they are still doing it in the Sudan and throughout most of Africa.

Why is it that in his description of his trip to the Sudan, 14 times during that description, Farrakhan mentioned that the people in the South were black, black, black as though there was some special kind of black. There is some special kind of black. They are blue-black; they are blue-velvety blacks, smooth black. They are the handsomest people I have ever laid my eyes on in all of my life. They wear it with pride, as though the deities did a special job on them. As though when the deity made the other people, he was rehearsing on how to make these people, but when he made those special Black people of the Sudan he had perfected his skill, and now he was putting his show on the road. However, his emphasis was as though their color was a detriment. I see it as an asset. Nobody is going to ever doubt who they are. When he mentioned the people in the North he said, "Well, they're mixed up, kind of just like us." Some of them are bastards, some are blacks calling themselves Arabs. My point here is that until we understand the African background to the tragedy, we will not understand that Africans coming to the United States against their will was just a variation of something that had been happening for more than a thousand years. When we hear about what the Romans and the Greeks did, we have to look at history critically. Africa would have been better off without the Roman and Greek connection; their total contribution to Africa was chaos and confusion.

This is why in order to aggrandize itself, to feed itself and to recover from the money spent on the Crusades and all the rest of the journeys outside of Europe, it recovered by the re-introduction of maritime skills, mostly taken from China. Europe started the Atlantic slave trade concurrent with the Arabs' destruction of East Africa with their slave trade.

The Arabs had finally bastardized a large part of the coast of East Africa by the cohabitation with African women. They had created a generation of Arabs that looked African and used them to start the East African slave trade. We now had the East African slave trade and the wrecking of the great city-states along East Africa, together with Europeans hitting West Africa, the slave trade from North Africa into West Africa, and later the invasion of South Africa where Europeans et al. did not take Africans out of Africa but enslaved them right at home. We would have been more effective in the fight against apartheid had we understood this was not just a fight against apartheid; this was a fight against chattel slavery, imposed on the spot.

We need to look at this picture and then look at the early nineteenth century conflict between Europeans over territory and the rise of the British abolitionists, who need to be studied separate and distinct from the British anti-slavery movement. The British abolitionists in a lot of cases were against slavery in England as such, but did not champion the freedom of a single slave in the slave trading colonies. They said, "All right, we can look at this dirty stuff and turn our back on it." William Pitt would say, "Have your slavery, that

is a weed that grows in every land; but don't bring
it here. Practice your dirty stuff away from home
and aggrandize your finances at home, but don't
bring it here." For its part, the British working
class — envious of the jobs that the slaves had in
Britain, which were often better than theirs —
began a campaign to get rid of the slaves and get
those jobs for themselves.

In 1807, the British effected a law to outlaw
slavery at sea. This began to deprive the United
States of a lot of their slave trading routes. To
combat this, the Americans built the Yankee
Clipper, a slave ship that could outrun the British
at sea. This led to the War of 1812. This
conflict would later make the British free their
slaves in the Caribbean Islands. Hear me clearly
now, go through a fake emancipation of people in
the Caribbean Islands that is not understood to this
day. When you compare it with emancipation in the
United States, that came thirty years later — and
that some black Americans argue the point, saying
"My fakery came thirty years before your fakery" —
because it was a fakery in both cases, it was not
emancipation in either case. It was a change in the
form of slavery, not emancipation because
emancipation has not taken place as yet, because
only the slave can free the slave.

In the Caribbean Islands the Africans were
allegedly free. They had no place to work, no place
to stay. They had to go back to the same
plantation to work; now they had to support their
families with a pittance, working on the same land.
So emancipation was a form of re-enslavement on
other terms, and the slave master got the best of
the terms. We are to this day washing our ego
with the assumption that something had taken place
that had not taken place at all. The indication
that it had not taken place is that by 1865, in
Jamaica, we had the Morant Bay confrontation,
and rebellion again. What were they rebelling
against if they were free? They were rebelling
against this new slavery; what Gordon is
talking about. This rebellion indicated their
realization that the emancipation had been a

141

farce and a fakery.

Now the Caribbean people in many of the islands, especially in Jamaica, began to confront this and take physical action against the system. On the island of Barbados they had the Bossie Revolt. Barbados had less revolts than other islands because Barbados is flat; and to have a successful revolt, in most cases, you really need hills, forests and riverbanks to use as a kind of shield. You can't match your enemy weapon for weapon; you just don't have the weaponry. However, if you know the forests and the hills, you've got a natural camouflage for protection. You can fight him with a minimum of weapons because many times you know where he is and he doesn't know where you are.

These gradually successful revolts and the fact that there were more and more skilled Caribbean craftsmen who worked their way out of indenture and could communicate with a similar class in the United States brought about more cooperation before the end of the nineteenth century. You had Caribbean people and African American people who understood something then they do not understand now: they've got the same enemy; it is the same system of oppression that oppresses both of them; it is the same system of economic robbery that robs both of them; it is the same system that doesn't give a damn about either of them.

All of this realization led to the concept, beginning in a formal sense in the Caribbean Islands, of Pan Africanism. This Pan African movement was a movement to liberate the mind. It had started in another way in the United States with the realization of our early writers, our anti-slavery orators and going back to a sense of trying to reclaim and look back at the Africa that had been lost. Now it started also with a relationship between the Caribbean freeman and the African American freeman. We were coming together now based on common need and common enemy, more then than now. Both of us formulated an independent church. Part of the activity of that church was based on the liberation of and ultimate return to

Africa on the large part of us.

What went wrong? Maybe the illusion before the alleged emancipation led to illusions after the emancipation. Mavis Campbell's work, *The Jamaican Coloreds, Social Political History, 1835-1885*, is very instructive. Mavis Campbell, as I have said before, is a competent researcher. Sometimes she's not the best personality because she is really a black Englishwoman of the nineteenth century, not the twentieth. Those are her values and she swears by certain British scholars who I have examined and found wanting, especially Christopher Fyffe and his work on Sierra Leone. Yet she has written five or six very competent books, including her book on the Maroons. She has done so much work on the Maroons she has declared ownership of them; she refers to them as, "my Maroons." She doesn't respect anybody's work on the Maroons except hers as being of any great lasting value.

Let's examine what went wrong in 1865 and after in the Caribbean Islands. In 1865, the mulattoes and half-breeds tried to make a deal with England for special treatment. When England failed to give them special treatment, they gave England the assurance that if they got their special treatment they would protect England against the wrath of the Blacks. When they didn't get the special treatment some of them threatened to join the Blacks and some did. This created a dilemma for England. So England gradually began to make some concessions for them to the point that England created several societies; this is a diabolical colonial skill. They created several societies for them based on shades of color: a brown society, an almost white society and a Black society at the bottom. To some extent, these societal strata still exist in the Jamaica of today.

That society led to a Jamaican myth called, "Out of many comes one." When they say out of many comes one, why is it that a Black one never ends up on top? Why is it that they would elect a Boston con man named Seaga and neglect some of the most brilliant Black men in the Caribbean Islands living

143

right there in their midst? Rhodes scholars, people who studied and mastered engineering, fine technicians. They would let the con man from Boston who stole them deaf, dumb and blind still walk around free without a scratch. Once they rid themselves of him they would go back to the high-yellow type, but the jet Black men haven't made it yet in the politics of Jamaica. What I'm saying is if I say that the aftermath of slavery was a new form of slavery in the Caribbean, it was the same in the United States.

In America they suffered the same thing but not quite as ruthlessly. United States slave masters didn't care too much about gradations of color, not even when he realized that some of the gradations were products of his own efforts. Some of the children were light enough to be sent to schools up North. Some were light enough to be sent to Edin-burgh, in Scotland. This is why after Emancipation our basic leadership, our congressmen, some of the people who headed our institutions, and some heads of our universities, were light complexioned. This was not a thing of design, but a larger number of them had the basic education to do those jobs. It took a generation to darken down the situation to the point where it became almost even-steven as to who would head our institutions without placing any great emphasis of consequence on complexion. Besides, some of the light-skinned were enlightened enough to turn the game on those who created the game. No one did it better than a brilliant white politician passing for Black named Adam Clayton Powell, Jr. He passed for Black, enjoyed every moment of it, and got the work done. He used less than one-tenth of his talent and got more work done than anybody we ever sent to Congress. A lot of our early college presidents came from that group. However, there was an illusion after Emancipation. We did not understand that our illusion led us into a new form of slavery. We had the illusion that we were free and that's why we were not free, because we bathed in the illusion and didn't face the reality. That was our problem right after the civil rights movement when we were betrayed by civil rights pimps, anti-poverty pimps, black studies pimps. We haven't dealt with these pimps to this day and they're still out there, living well. They take advantage of the fact that we think we are free and play on this situation.

In the United States, after the alleged Emancipation, we had access to public office. There were probably more mayors in the South then than we have right now. We were the majority in some legislatures, yet the one thing that was happening to the man furthest down, the working people, was the fact that the land had been confiscated. There wasn't enough land, and we were reduced to sharecropping, peonage and the worst jobs in the South that were the worst paying. Land is the basis of nationhood at home and away from home. Away from home the possession of land preserves your Nationhood Frame of Mind. So once again the aftermath of slavery was a form of slavery. Just like the aftermath of colonialism is another form of colonialism. These are things we haven't sat down and discussed.

We haven't sat down and discussed that the state that came after was modeled after the people who destroyed the original African state. They could not see that we had justice in our society before their interference, and without a single civil lawyer. The elders in our family were the equivalent of the Supreme Court. We had better justice than any democratic nation in the world, in most cases, with no political parties. The first thing your colonial masters destroyed was your system of arbitration. When you have a system of arbitration among yourselves, you have a way of settling disputes among yourselves without their interference — you've got something better than their justice system. When you throw that away and adopt their system of civil justice, you have re-enslaved yourself to them.

This is why I had asked Brother Richard Berry to locate a book for me on the Australian aborigines. Among the many things I am doing is preparing a book for our young on *The Africans Away From Home*. The intent of the book is to instruct them on how to locate themselves on the map of human geography. African people can be found in India. What were we doing there? African people can be found in Australia. How did we get there? And what did we do before so-called civilization was forced on us? How do we handle the word "civilization" without analyzing the word "civil"? How is it that so many people who refer to themselves as civilized are not civil? Once you define the word "civil" you'll find that what you call civilization doesn't match up with it. The beginning of the word varies depending on who it is applied to.

With the present enthusiasm of blacks in public office, we seem to have forgotten that land is the basis of nationhood. Very few of them are doing anything to preserve our right to preserve the land in Africa and the land we need to sustain ourselves away from home. To be land dependent is another form of slavery; freedom and dependency are not compatible. During the period after slavery, we had a lot of land thanks to the promises of certain enlightened congressmen and senators. Some said give us the land and let us make our own way; some said give us the boat and let us make our way out of here. However, we did have some sympathetic friends. Once they were eliminated from power, we didn't have any friends left in Congress, and gradually blacks were pushed out of Congress, and out of local legislatures.

Near the end of the century we had no strong voices in Congress. The few that were left were not even paid much attention to. So we come now to the year 1895. Whites got tired of listening to a multiplicity of leaders, so they chose one and white editorial writers have been choosing our leaders ever since. They chose Booker T. Washington, but don't ever judge Booker T. Washington as being just an "uncle tom." He was also a strategist whose strategy didn't always work. I have said repeatedly he'd scratch his head when nothing itched and he shuffled his feet when he didn't want to dance; he said "yes" when he didn't want to say yes so that another generation could say, "Hell No." However, when you became strong enough to say "Hell No," you did not take advantage of the strength you should have had because of his sacrifice to move you to this juncture in history.

I am saying that you failed him. By his bowing and scraping, he was trying to prepare you so you wouldn't have to bow and scrape. We still haven't understood him yet. We keep thinking that there was a fight between Du Bois and Washington; there was no fight — there was a difference of opinion. Before his Atlanta Cotton Exposition speech, although he was the keynote speaker, he entered through a Jim Crow door and waited in a Jim Crow section until it was his time to speak. Psychologically he was still a slave just like the rest of us. After that speech he changed this nation; he had given new direction to this nation. He made a concession, called a compromise, that was a strategic move, a holding action, hopefully to give us time to get ourselves together. This is why you don't understand him and you don't understand Martin Luther King.

Martin Luther King in his preaching of the concept of non-violence bought us the time to prepare to be violent. Understand him in that light and stop thinking of him as teaching us to be cowards. Had we been violent at the time, it would have been suicide because we didn't have anything but our hands and they weren't even good enough. However, he gave us the time to think it out. "If we're going to fight, where are we going to get guns? If we're going to hide, where are we going to hide?" You want to talk revolution, how do we understand the nature of revolution. To understand the aftermath of struggle, you have to understand the nature of the pressure against those who are struggling against the condition. Don't judge people just at once.

I have heard people say right here in this room, and I've heard one of Marcus Garvey's sons say the same thing, "I've never read anything by Du Bois and I never will. I have no intention of reading anything he wrote." If you have not read W.E.B. Du Bois' little essay, "Pan Africanism: A Mission of My Life," six printed pages, I'm willing to question your right to speak about Pan Africanism. If you have not read his towering masterpiece, *Black Reconstruction in America, 1860 - 1880*, I question your knowledge of what happened to Black people after the Civil War and the alleged end of slavery. Again within that same book is an essay, which needs to be printed separately and circulated around the world, called "The Propaganda of History."

Had we turned to ourselves for some kind of understanding, we would have realized what was let loose after our alleged emancipation. We witnessed the rise of the Ku Klux Klan and related secret societies. The poor class whites feared that we would have a status that would threaten their status. They were not slave holders; they didn't make a lot of money. Here the slave was emerging with more skills than they had.

Remember during slavery the slave developed a lot of building skills, leather tanning skills, etc. Now these skills were paying partially decent salaries. There were a lot of poor whites without these skills; and because they lacked the nerve to fight the whites who put them into this bind, they fought us. People still fight us as a substitute for confronting their real enemy, and we suffer from not being able to identify our real enemy. And because we do not understand the nature of this kind of struggle, we, instead of fighting them, turn on each other. We turn on each other based on who came from what speck of dust in the Caribbean Sea called an island. We turn on each other based on who came from what speck of dust in America. The slave ships brought no Barbadians, brought no Jamaicans, no Deltas, no AKAs, no Africans with a color problem. All of the Africans in this forced migration were the victims of the same tragedy, with variations. We have got to understand the nature of these variations. We should never talk about each other because we're from different parts of the world of oppression. We should never

148

separate ourselves because we came from different parts of the world of oppression. We should never say that somebody else from that other part is not of our culture. If you are not talking about African culture, you are not talking about anything. We could easily settle the differences between us based on this realization.

At the end of the nineteenth century, all of us in the world had been engaged in a massive struggle for some kind of personal and national sovereignty. The African mind was being influenced by the missionary-trained African. For one hundred years the Africans did not negotiate anything; they took their spears and their shields and went to the field of battle and out-maneuvered some of the best military minds of Europe. Winston Churchill bears witness to this in an excellent book called, *The River War*. Missionary-trained Africans had begun to take over and communicate with Europeans. They began to appeal to the conscience of the European, not knowing where power is concerned and where the European is concerned, there is no conscience to appeal to. There are no "Thou-shall -nots" in their approach to African people.

These missionary-trained Africans, these nationalists, manifested themselves best in South Africa, Ghana, Nigeria and partly in Uganda. In West Africa they created something that had not been created in the other parts of Africa in quite the same way: a great national literature of liberation, which has not been read or fully appreciated to this very day. Casely Hayford, the political father of the politics of modern Ghana, wrote *Ethiopia Unbound, The Truth About the West African Land Problem*, and *Native Institutions*. These works were followed by books like *Toward Nationhood in West Africa, West Africa at the Bar of Justice*, and other works by West African writers. A great traditionalist, John Mensah Sarbah, wrote *Fanti Customary Law* and *Fanti Law and Constitution*. Sarbah was the mentor of Casely Hayford. Hayford was the mentor of Joseph B. Danquah, who was subsequently the mentor of Kwame Nkrumah.

More than anything else the nation that was going to become Ghana again had created a literature of liberation that explained why, in spite of years of occupation, they never accepted the fact that a foreigner had a right to rule them; they never let their mind dwell on that fact. This is explained so beautifully in a classic essay by Danquah called, "The Fanti Bond of 1844." We have not read this literature. People go to Ghana, buy kente cloth, grin and skin, eat Ghanaian food and don't read one page of one book. If it were left to me, that would be a requirement for going to any country in Africa. You would have to read at least three books on the country before you were allowed in. I don't think I would make a very welcomed dictator because I would do it too well. I understand some things, if they are to exist, will have to be dictated and you have got to throw the nonsense in the garbage can. Now, because we have not understood this, we have not made the best use of our liberation movements.

At the end of the nineteenth century in Africa, their military-trained Africans were taking over the independence struggle. At the end of the nineteenth century in the Caribbean Islands, you had something a little more enlightening. You had the Pan African League being developed into a Pan African Congress. We have this movement that is being brought into being mostly by Trinidadians like H. Sylvester Williams, George Padmore and C.L.R. James. Look at the irony. This nation, Trinidad, brought into being three major Pan Africanists and yet the Pan African idea did not even get across to the Trinidadians. They missed the best points of some of their finest thinkers. This is true of the entire Caribbean. Right today, if Garvey went to Jamaica alive, with his Black self, he might be stoned to death. They are not buying any Blackness in Jamaica, no Pan Africanism, or African nationalism either. The Rastas, with their politically mixed-up selves, came closer to it than anybody else. They think Haile Selassie is their god, but they haven't seriously studied Haile Selassie. Haile Selassie is not only not a god, he is not even a pure Ethiopian; but that's another subject. However, the Rasta did make a step toward Africa, a step toward some kind of self-reliance. I don't think they are hopeless, but I see too many of them scattered throughout the Caribbean complementing their scanty incomes by fulfilling the desires of sexually starved white women on the beach. I just don't think the road to Africa leads in that direction, and they are missing the point, too.

In the United States after the oppression of slavery, segregation and the partial attempt to eliminate it, we made the wrong move. In the fight for integration when Eisenhower said, "With all deliberate speed," this slowed down everything. They didn't mean it in the first place. Segregation was a form of slavery and oppression. In the Caribbean the form of British domination and the lessening of that domination was based on the radical demand for the land. There was British Crown land and Reserve land, while there were people right there on the island with not even enough land to grow a tomato. This fight for the land, which did not start among the aristocratic Jamaicans, started among the common Jamaicans, the common people of the island. What happened to the land? You've got land here called Reserves; if I want to grow a tomato on it, I can't. According to Colonial Law how can someone else's land become Crown land or be called Reserves? It was this fight for access to the land that started the fight for real independence. It did not start among Caribbean aristocrats and those with an education; it started among very common people. Why do these aristocrats come up and take credit for things they did not do? Then they take the common people, the same common people who fought for them, and neglect their needs while they accept corruption and build houses in the hills and look down on the very people who made their living conditions possible.

The same can be said about this country. The same people who we opened doors for, later closed doors for the others. Except for the Civil Rights Movement and affirmative action, a Clarence Thomas wouldn't be on the Supreme Court and he wouldn't be

151

living in the suburbs of Washington with a white wife. Skip Gates wouldn't be living in the suburbs of Boston with his white wife because he wouldn't be at Harvard University in the first place. Why can't we let some of these people know this? Why can't we let them know that the aftermath of that form of oppression was a form of slavery itself? Why is it that now a concentrated effort is being made by whites to spread as much dissension as they can among Caribbean people, African American people and African people? Why are we fool enough to fall for it? Why don't we understand that this is misconception, one to the other, and the road back to chattel slavery. If we get too deeply involved in this dilemma, we're not going to be able to get out because the next time it's going to be computerized. Ain't no way out of that one. We have to settle down and close some doors and stop all of the nonsense and mythology of integration. We have some serious problems to take care of within our house, and we better close our door to make sure only the family is in the house and get these problems taken care of.

Why do we have to always insist, "Well, we got one of our Hispanic brothers here, and one of our Dominican brothers is here." Do you understand that the Dominicans are literally reducing the Haitians to slavery and using child labor on the island they share in the Caribbean? They are right here in our own community running stores and a whole lot of black women are sleeping with Dominicans so that their children can have a different texture of hair and a lighter color. They are sleeping with Arabs for the same reason. Why is the black woman so precious now that she can't be criticized? And why is she so open to criticize anybody she wants to? And are we supposed to look the other way while she commits equally as much sin against our progress as the men are committing?

We are both wrong. This is why I resented the concept of atonement at the Million Man March on Washington. What are we atoning for? She didn't come here on no separate slave ship; she didn't have a separate auction block. We were together in oppression. She performed some miracles that literally saved us, and we have acknowledged that. We had to survive on what white people threw away. We were not a great pork-eating people in Africa, but here in this country we made delicacies out of hog's feet, out of his guts, out of his head — things white people didn't eat. There used to be a time when white people didn't eat liver. We could buy ten cents worth of liver; and with some rice and some greens, we could feed ten or twelve people. For ten cents. The Black woman in that kitchen was manipulating all these different things.

We have used some survival tools that kept us on this earth and now we're turning our back on them, acting as though we're ashamed of them, and they are what kept us here. We can't divide ourselves between man and woman because we have the same basic problems in the same society. Alice Walker and some other misguided fools like Terry McMillan are giving you some illusions. However, those illusions don't tell you that nobody made any place for you in other societies; you better come home and make peace because you ain't got no other place to go. Black women have no place to go permanently without Black men, and Black men have no place to go permanently without Black women. We ain't got no place to go without you; you ain't got no other place to go without us. So when I say to you the aftermath of slavery is a new form of slavery, this is what I'm talking about.

Your illusion about your position in relationship to white people is no different now than it was then. They will sleep with you, use you, but they do not want you as a permanent part of their society. All of us need to learn this, O.J. needs to learn this and Alice Walker needs to learn this, too. We will survive as one people, united, or we won't survive at all. There is no capitalist solution for our problem because capitalism got its seed money, its jump start, from our enslavement and the exploitation of our communities. You can't use the same system to save you that enslaved you; there is a difference between Pan Capitalism and Pan Africanism.

153

In Pan Capitalism, the cooperation is based on super profit, and you've got to have a large number of people who work for low wages or no wages at all. Pan Africanism takes us back to the kind of consumer collective society that produced us in the first place where the ruler of the state was not the owner of the wealth, but the guardian of the wealth. This kind of society existed in Africa not only before Karl Marx, but before Europe. If you do not understand this, then you have some confusion between the Karl Marxes and the Groucho Marxes. We have to understand that a social system that is successful with other people is not necessarily a success with us; because it is a success with only one level of their people, it can be fatal among their people, too. Remember when the British were building their empire, a lot of Englishmen were so poor they were eating out of garbage cans. So the capitalist system has always been unfair because it has never been balanced. The only thing that can be balanced is a collective society. If a society is collective, its people receive goods and services according to their needs, as opposed to their ability to pay, if they're part of the totality of the society; and they contribute the best they can based on their ability. You do not deny them basic human services because someone else has more ability than they have. If a family has six children to feed and another has two children to feed, the larger family gets enough food to feed six children regardless of the fact that the family who has two children to feed might have more ability. That's humanness; that's humaneness.

Remember, there is something we have to start concentrating on and get back to. Unless we use it well and understand it well, we might perish under the present political climate. How did we behave in Africa? How did we survive out of Africa when we were at our best? We did ask the question, either silently or verbally, that every conscious people must ask: how will my people stay on this earth? If you ask that question right now, you'll stop asking for jobs and you'll begin to create jobs. If you ask the question, how will my people stay on this earth, you'll say, "Well, they wear shoes. Who's going to make them?" If you make them, you're creating jobs. "They wear underwear. Who's going to make them?" You make them and you're creating a textile industry. "Who's going to feed them?" You? You're creating an agricultural industry. This, all by asking a single set of questions. Then there is another question that you must also ask. You must ask this of every leader. If he can't answer the question to your satisfaction, remove him from power at once. The question is: leader, where are you leading me? And if I don't want to go that way, then you're not my leader. Have you consulted me first to see if I want to go that way?

What we are doing is engaging in a form of mind liberation that keeps you out of the prey of hustlers, foreigners, fakers and fools. Then you can begin to understand what we did when we were at our best. When we were building Egypt, we would send down that Nile River a cadre of civilizers that would build Egypt. Along with this we had something that we had better get back to if we are going to survive: high morality and collective discipline. With collective discipline we created collective security, not individuality that ignored the person. We knew that the good of one and the good of all was basically the same and that we had to protect each other in order to protect the totality of the people. There wasn't any argument about it. We didn't argue about who was a Baptist or who was a Protestant or who was a Holy Roller. We recognized who was a human being with a right of choice; this was in a personal area.

Now we have a faker who is going to bring us into an Islamic superpower. Nothing could be more detrimental to us in this world than a religious enslaver. This would be detrimental to any people. It is detrimental to everyone. Nothing is more ruthless than a religious enslaver.

You studied Europe under feudalism, before the Protestant Reformation. Understand what I'm talking about. It was a capitalistic dictatorship. You weren't allowed to be anything other than a Catholic and you were told who to obey and what to obey. Martin Luther's revolt saved the church because once he revolted and told the people there were other choices, some people stayed in the Catholic church but on different terms. The Catholic church then was forced to be more reasonable. It was a contribution. Although I think Martin Luther was a confused schizophrenic, he did open that door and introduced the possibility that there could have been another way. But when you've got only one way to approach God, only one way to communicate with God, you've got different prices you have to pay in order for someone to communicate for you. If they raised the price, based on something called purgatory, someone had to take a principled stand. "There must be another way to do this." I don't think Martin Luther was the clearest person in his own approach, but he did open the door for the possibility of a dialogue.

What I'm asking you to do in the final analysis is to guard against the new form of slavery that is approaching and stop all of these nonsensical arguments among yourselves: the who came from what part of what geography, the who came from Africa, the who came from what island, the who came from Georgia, etc. In the end we all have the same enemy and we all have to face that enemy. We have to rebuild our institutions and realize that we are rich people who are making poor use of our riches.

With the money taken in at the Million Man March, we could have saved one of our predominantly Black colleges. Yet we are not even supposed to be asking questions about the amount collected and what was done with it. If it's about us, we are the first people who should be asking the questions. We have a person going around the world in a first-rate airplane, with a well-paid flight crew of six at least, an entourage of thirty, staying in classy hotels. With that same money we could have saved another predominantly Black college or built one. With the sale of one of the stretch limousines of the leader, you could have seen a Black child through medical school. But we have not asked that

question: leader, where are you leading me? Then
let us ask: where is the money? The Black
Baptist church takes up more money than six European
nations and they don't own a shoeshine parlor.

What you have to do about leadership is to look
in the mirror and understand that you have some
responsibility for their poor leadership. Say to
yourself, as Ron Daniels has said, "We are the
leaders that we have been looking for."

Unless we are alert to all of the things I
have mentioned, chances are, we will be the
victims of another form of slavery still to come.
Tomorrow, it has been said, belongs to those who
prepare for it. First and foremost, we need to
be prepared to save ourselves.

John Henrik Clarke
First World Lecture Series
New York, New York
March 30, 1996

CONTRIBUTORS

JOHN HENRIK CLARKE, born in Union Springs, Alabama, is a historian, a teacher, a writer, a lecturer and a book reviewer. From his early years he studied the history of African people and received the first license to teach African and African American history in New York. He is presently Professor Emeritus of African World History at Hunter College. Dr. Clarke is a world-renown lecturer and has edited and written over twenty-five books on African and African American history, culture, and politics. The best known being, *African People At The Crossroads: Notes for an African World Revolution, Christopher Columbus and the Afrikan Holocaust, Malcolm X: The Man and His Times,* and *Marcus Garvey and the Vision of Africa.* As a writer of fiction he has published over fifty short stories, the best known being, "The Boy Who Painted Christ Black."

LLOYD BEST, a native of Trinidad, was educated at Downing College, Cambridge and Mansfield College, Oxford. He served as a fellow of the Institute of Social and Economic Research at the University of the West Indies in Trinidad, a research associate at the Ecole Pratique des Hautes Etudes of the University of Paris, and taught at the University of Puerto Rico. Best was an economic planning consultant to the government of Trinidad and Tobago, and is a frequent consultant on the economy of the West Indies and a respected authority on the economic development of the Caribbean area.

STAUGHTON LYND has had a distinguished career as a teacher of history and as a discerning writer and commentator on the colonial period in America, on the American Revolution and the early national period, on slavery and abolitionism, and on American foreign policy. He was educated at Harvard and Columbia Universities and taught at Spelman College, in Atlanta, at Yale University and at the Industrial Areas Foundation Training Institute in Chicago.

159

Both a scholar and a libertarian, his published works include *Class Conflict, Slavery, and the United States Constitution*; *Reconstruction*; *Intellectual Origins of American Radicalism*; and his best known work, *A People History of the United States*.

EDGAR A. TOPPIN has had a scholarly career characterized not only by his outstanding publications but by his deep concern for African American rights and history. The three main books he wrote were devoted to the American Black heritage. *Pioneers and Patriots* depicts the lives of six Blacks of the Revolutionary era while *A Mark Well Made* outlines Black contributions to American culture. *The Unfinished March* analyzes the African American from Reconstruction to World War I.

Professor Toppin received his Ph.D from Northwestern University. He taught at Alabama State College, Fayetteville State College, and Virginia State College.

STERLING STUCKEY is well known for his advocacy of African American history as a subject for scholarly concern. As part of his deep commitment to integrate Black Studies into our educational system, Mr. Stuckey wrote many articles, participated in many symposiums and has belonged to many groups dealing with the subject.

One of his many articles that was widely distributed was, "The Place of Black Studies in the Curriculum." His best known books are *Slave Culture: Nationalist Theory and Foundation of Black America,* and *The Ideological Origins of Black Nationalism.*

BIBLIOGRAPHY

Aptheker, Herbert. *A Documentary History of the Negro in the United States*, Vol. 1. New York: Citadel Press, reissued 1969.

_____. *American Negro Slave Revolts*. New York: International Publishers, 1963.

Bennett, Lerone, Jr. *Before the Mayflower*. Baltimore: Penquin Press, 1966.

_____. *The Challenge of Blackness*. Chicago: Johnson Publishing Co., 1972.

Blanshard, Paul. *Democracy and Empire in the Caribbean*. New York: McMillan Publishing Co., 1947.

Blassingame, John. *The Slave Community*. New York: Oxford University Press, 1979.

Blyden, Edward W. *Christianity, Islam and the Negro Race*. Edinburgh: Edinburgh University Press, 1967.

Boahen, A. Adu. "The Coming of the Europeans," in *The Horizon History of Africa*. New York: American Heritage Publishing, 1971.

_____. with Ajayi, J.F. Ade and Tidy, Michael. *Topics in West African History*. Essex, England: Longman Group Ltd, 1986.

Bradley, Michael. *The Columbus Conspiracy*. New York: A&B Books, 1992.

Clarke, John H. *Slave Trade and Slavery*. New York: Holt, Rinehart & Winston, 1970.

_____. *Christopher Columbus and the Afrikan Holocaust*. New York: A&B Books, 1992.

Coupland, Sir Reginald. *The British Anti-Slavery Movement*. London: Frank Cass & Co. Ltd., 1964.

_____. *East Africa and Its Invaders*. London: Oxford University Press, 1938.

Curry, Richard. *The Abolitionists*. New York: Holt Rinehart & Winston, 1965.

Davidson, Basil. *A History of West Africa to the Nineteenth Century*. New York: Anchor Books, Doubleday and Co., 1966.

_____. *Black Mother: The Years of the African Slave Trade: Precolonial History, 1450-1850*. Boston: Atlantic-Little, Brown & Co., 1961.

_____. *The Black Man's Burden: The Curse of the Nation-State*. New York: Times Books, Random House, 1992.

de Las Casas, Bartolome. *The Devastation of the Indies: A Brief Account*. New York: Seabury Press, 1971.

Dobler, Livinia and Toppin, Edgar A. *Pioneers and Patriots*. New York: Zenith Books, Doubleday and Co., 1965.

Duberman, Martin. *The Anti-Slavery Vanguard*. Princeton: Princeton University Press, 1965.

Elkins, Stanley. *Slavery: A Problem in American Institutional and Intellectual Life*. New York: Grossett & Dunlap, 1983.

Filler, Louis. *History of the People of the United States from Revolution to Civil War*. New York: Noonday Press. 1964.

Franklin, John Hope. *From Slavery to Freedom.* New York: Vintage Books, Random House, 1969.

Gayle, Addison, Jr. *Black Expression.* New York: Weybright & Tally, 1969.

Genovese, Eugene D. *The Political Economy of Slavery.* New York: Pantheon Books, 1965.

Howard, Warren S. *American Slavers & Federal Law, 1837-1862.* Davis: University of California Press, 1963.

Human Rights Watch. *Children of Sudan: Slaves, Street Children and Child Soldiers.* New York: 1995.

Inikore, Joseph E. *Forced Migration.* New York: Americana Publishers, 1974.

Johnston, Sir Harry. *The Colonization of Africa by Alien Races.* London: Cambridge University Press, 1913.

Jordan, Winthrop D. *White Over Black.* Chapel Hill: University of North Carolina, 1968.

Klein, Herbert S. *Slavery in the Americas.* Chicago: University of Chicago Press, 1967.

Lester, Julius. *To Be A Slave.* New York: Dial Press, 1968.

Lewis, Bernard. *The Arabs In History.* New York: Colophone Books, Harper and Row, 1966.

Logan, Rayford Whittingham. *The Negro in the United States, A Brief History.* Princeton, NJ: Van Nostrand Books, 1947.

May, F. George. *The Shameful Trade.* Cranbury, NJ: A.S. Barnes, 1967.

McManus, Edgar S. *A History of Negro Slavery in New York*. Syracuse, NY: Syracuse University Press, 1966.

Nelson, Truman. *The Right of Revolution*. Boston: Beacon Press, 1968.

Newton, A.P. *The European Nations in the West Indies, 1493-1688*. New York: Barnes and Noble, 1967.

Quarles, Benjamin. *The Negro in the Making of America*. New York: Collier Books, 1964.

_____. *The Negro in the American Revolution*. Chapel Hill, NC: Chapel Hill Books, University of North Carolina Press, 1961.

_____. *Black Abolitionists*. New York: Oxford University Press, 1969.

Redding, Saunders. *They Came in Chains*. New York: Lippincott Press, 1950.

Richames, Louis. *The Abolitionists*. New York: Putnam Books, 1963.

Stampp, Kenneth. *The Peculiar Institution*. New York: Vintage Books, Random House, 1964.

Sterling, Philip and Logan, Rayford. *Four Took Freedom*. New York: Zenith Books, Doubleday and Co., 1967.

Stuckey, Sterling. *Slave Culture: Nationalist Theory and the Foundations of Black America*. New York: Oxford University Press, 1987.

Tannenbaum, Frank. *Slave and Citizen: The Negro in the Americas*. New York: Vintage Books, Random House, 1946.

Thoreau, Henry David. *Anti-Slavery and Reform Papers*. Montreal: Harvest House, 1963.

Washington, Booker T. *Up From Slavery.* New York: Dell Books, 1965.

Weinstein, Allen and Gatell, Frank Otto. *American Negro Slavery: A Modern Reader.* New York: Oxford University Press, 1969.

Wesley, Charles H. *Neglected History.* Wilberforce, OH: Central State College Press, 1965.

Williams, Eric. *Capitalism and Slavery.* New York: Capricorn Books, 1966.

_____. *British Historians and the West Indies.* Port of Spain, Trinidad: PNM Publishing Co., 1964.

_____. *Documents of West Indian History 1492-1655.* Port of Spain, Trinidad: PNM Publishing Co., 1963.

_____. *History of the People of Trinidad and Tobago.* Port of Spain, Trinidad: PNM Publishing Co., 1962.

Woodward, C. Vann. *The Burden of Southern History.* Baton Rouge: Louisiana State University Press, 1968.

Zilversmit, Arthur. *The First Emancipation: The Abolition of Slavery in the North.* Chicago: University of Chicago Press, 1967.

INDEX

Reader's Index

Reader's Index

Reader's Index